THESE
WATCHED HIM DIE

THESE
WATCHED HIM DIE

LESLIE HARDINGE

REVIEW AND HERALD® PUBLISHING ASSOCIATION
Since 1861 | www.reviewandherald.com

This book was
Designed by Ron J. Pride
Cover art: Review and Herald Art Library
Typeset: Bembo 12/15

PRINTED IN U.S.A.

13 12 11 10 09   5 4 3 2 1

Library of Congress Cataloging-in-Publication Data

Hardinge, Leslie, 1912-2002.
   These watched him die   /   Leslie Hardinge
        128 p. 22 cm.
     1. Jesus Christ—Crucifixion.
I. Title.
     BT450 .H26
     232.963
                    66019415

ISBN 978-0-8280-2422-8

To my daughter

Judy

and all the young in heart

to whom I would reveal

JESUS

in His loving compassion

I dedicate this book

Contents

Introduction

All humanity was gathered at the cross. All humanity made final decisions in its shadow.

The story of the Crucifixion is a microcosm of the last judgment. The persons who clustered about the dying Savior were representatives of us all. As we think of these people and consider what made them what they were, let us recognize that they mirror our thoughts and feelings and dispositions. Their varied attitudes represent our own reactions.

They gathered about the crosses, these faceless ones, attracted there by the morbid feelings that impel men to witness executions. Some stood and stared stolidly. Some moved uneasily, emotionally involved in the agony of dying men. Others impassively watched the soldiers methodically going about their grisly task of ceremonially ending three lives. Then there were those who seemed to be enjoying the sights and sounds of a blood-mad crowd. Their satisfaction sprang from feelings of vengeance. Justice was being met! A traitor, a murderer, a brigand, were receiving due recompense for their crimes.

The Romans were there. Their role was to see that Caesar's might was felt and Caesar's laws were carried out to the letter. No question as to Rome's authority might be raised with impunity when they were around! As procurator of Judea, Pilate bore the authority of Tiberius himself. His judgment was final. He had acted. The law, as he interpreted it, was being enforced.

The centurion was there with his soldiers. They were getting some satisfaction in thinking of the perquisites they would receive. They sat down under the cross to wait it out. As the blood fell, they cast lots for old clothes, and perhaps wondered how quickly they could get to the pawnbroker with their loot.

Herod was there in spirit. The Herods held a position that was complicated. They were part of the Roman government, and yet they were natives of Palestine. As Edomites they were hated by the Jews, but as benefactors, one of whom had rebuilt the Temple in Jerusalem on a lavish scale, they were tolerated by the people. Licentious and cruel, politic and callous, the Herods had slain the babes of Bethlehem and the Baptist in the dungeon. Herod Antipas must have gained sadistic satisfaction in the ending of a virtuous life by which his vice was condemned.

The Sanhedrin was there. Caiaphas, and possibly Annas, and chief representatives postured in the forefront of the crowd. These men stood for the religious power of their nation. They were the guardians of faith and morals. No query regarding God and His law, worship, or ritual might be mooted without opposition while they were around. No question of orthodoxy, which they upheld, was ever permitted. Their views had been criticized by this Nazarene. Their popularity with the people had waned because of His deeds. Their power and prestige were in jeopardy because of His life. As they watched Jesus being nailed ignominiously to a cross they gloated that the cause of their discomfort was being removed forever.

His companions in death were there. The thieves, receiving the just deserts for their deeds, were resisting the soldiers and seeking relief by cursing their executioners. They were obviously guilty, and few in the crowd felt sorry for them.

The disciples were there. Ashamed and scared, some of them

had slunk back to the place of the execution. John was nearest to the cross. Ardent and helpless, he stood close by. Alone, his heart was seeking the peace of forgiveness in solitude in the multitude. Mary of Bethany was at the foot of the cross. But gifts of love and tears of grief were impotent now. Mary of Nazareth, with her mother heart breaking, was watching her hopes and ambitions, her thoughtfulness and devotion, being extinguished with each passing moment by the cross. This was that to which Simeon had referred when he said, "Yea, a sword shall pierce through thy own soul also" (Luke 2:35).

And then there were people, people everywhere. Faces, nameless faces of anonymous people, coming and going. Shouting and laughing, confronted by the most solemn issues that humanity had ever faced, would ever face, they ambled childishly, thoughtlessly, in holiday mood at the foot of the cross.

All men and women stood around the cross that day. All men and women were in its shadow deciding for eternity as the Son of God was being executed. You and I were there. You and I are there. And in our watching today, we settle, without any question, the final destiny that will one day be ours.

Chapter 1

Simon the Conscripted

African Farmer—"He Bore the Cross"

Jesus stood before the governor with His back torn and lacerated by the scourge. Then Pilate the cowardly washed his hands of the whole affair. Shrugging to a soldier to do as the priests wished, the governor left Jesus to His fate and went to breakfast. With the blood-drunk crowd and the soldiers our Lord staggered out of the judgment hail on His way to Old Skull Face to be crucified.

As they started out, the executioners tried to force Him to carry His cross. He fell fainting under its weight. They probably threw some water over His face. When He felt better, they dragged Him up and put the cross on Him once more. Down He fell, and they tried to revive Him again. A man in the crowd expressed his sympathy. His name was Simon.

Simon, the farmer, was a stranger. He had come from Cyrene in North Africa. What had brought him to Palestine we are not told. The Gospel writer informs us that he had two boys, Alexander and Rufus (Mark 15:21). Perhaps this Rufus is the one to whom Paul sent greetings in the last chapter of Romans. But this we do not know for certain. We are told nothing of Simon's wife (Rom. 16:13), but she might have been in Jerusalem with her husband. This stranger, this North African, found himself on Passover day coming into Jerusalem from his field outside the city. Passing through the open gate, he met the huge crowd noisily moving out. He was suddenly surrounded by the cruel mob, bent on murder. He stopped and watched the cross laid upon the broken shoulders of a dying Man. He shuddered as He collapsed under the load. "He hears the taunts and ribaldry of the crowd; he hears the words contemptuously repeated, Make way for the King of the Jews! He stops in astonishment at the scene; and as he expresses his compassion, they seize him and place the cross upon his shoulders" (*The Desire of Ages*, p. 742). Because he voiced his sympathy, he was immediately commandeered to carry the instrument of torture himself.

Simon has heard about Jesus. While his two sons, Alexander and Rufus, had decided to accept Jesus as the Messiah (*ibid.*), Simon himself "had not (yet) openly professed faith in Christ" (*Early Writings*, p. 175). Had he been challenged he might well have declared himself a follower.

And so Simon, the African, finds himself suddenly conscripted into royal service. He was a helper of the King. I wonder whether he realized his privilege! Everyone in Palestine had heard about John's declaration that Jesus was the Messiah. Did Simon sense the contribution he was making in bringing the ministry of the Savior to its consummation?

But Simon had no choice in the matter. He had been conscripted. They had forcibly laid the cross upon him. As he staggered under its weight, the One who was to die upon it stumbled by his side. Around Simon men jeered. Ribald jokes and foolish banter were on many tongues. The air was filled with angry shouts. With the cross on his back Simon was alone with his thoughts. "His sympathies were deeply stirred in favor of Jesus; and the events of Calvary, and the words uttered by the Savior, caused him to acknowledge that He was the Son of God" (*The SDA Bible Commentary,* Ellen G. White Comments, on Matt. 27:32, p. 1107).

"The bearing of the cross to Calvary was a blessing to Simon, and he was ever after grateful for this providence. It led him to take upon himself the cross of Christ from choice, and ever cheerfully stand beneath its burden" (*The Desire of Ages*, p. 742).

I often think of the wonderful circumstances that had brought Simon to where he was at that time. His home was in Africa. But he had taken a dirty, inconvenient journey to Palestine. The dusty tracks of Libya, the sandy pathways across the Nile Valley, and the desert rocks of the coastal region were passed in turn. Crossing the highlands of the wilderness of Judea, he had come at last to the environs of Jerusalem. Somewhere near he had obtained a job. He had worked hard to support his sons, and perhaps his wife. He was a stranger in a strange land.

And then that Friday morning he trudged in from the fields outside Jerusalem. Here he met Jesus on His way to His sacrifice on the hill of execution. Had he reached that spot on the road five minutes earlier, he would have slipped into the gate unobserved, and perhaps we would never have heard about him. Five minutes later and the procession would have passed on its way to Calvary, and the executioners would have started on their grisly work. But he was neither five minutes early nor five minutes late. He was there at the right moment.

After His condemnation Jesus had passed on a little way from Pilate's judgment hall—possibly in the Castle of Antonia. Perhaps His fainting had occurred while He stumbled along the Pavement. Today the pilgrims bow low to kiss what might well be those very stones. They have been worn smooth and polished by the lips of unnumbered pious persons during the past 15 centuries, since Helena, Constantine's mother, made pilgrimages to holy places fashionable. Perhaps Jesus saw, carved in the Pavement itself, the games of the soldiers played with dice.

Simon took in the whole scene. Simon's heart was full of pity, and Simon's tongue spoke what Simon's heart felt. And as he spoke in sympathy he was conscripted by the soldiers. Perhaps he had at first wondered, Why didn't I keep my mouth closed? Perhaps someone in the crowd had shouted, "That goes for talking too much!" Whatever he thought, he carried the cross to Calvary and laid it down for Christ where the soldiers told him to.

Simon watched the executioners wrestle with the brigands. He shuddered as the Prisoner, whom he had helped, lay down voluntarily and stretched out His arms. He heard the sickening blow as the executioner's maul drove the spike through the bloody hand. His heart was torn by the sobbing of the mother. He heard the prayer, such as no man had ever prayed, "Father, forgive them; for they know not what they do." Did he feel that he was included in that petition? Did he sense a sudden increase of light? Had he, too, failed to understand what he had done when he had borne, perhaps resentfully at first, the cross to the place? Was he now learning that he too needed forgiveness? Did he remember the skepticism of yesterday, when he had heard the gospel and refused to obey? Did he recall the look in his sons' faces when they had eagerly affirmed, "Dad, this Man is the Messiah!" and he had refused to surrender? I like to think Christ's prayer embraced him, too. He was very near the cross. His was a grandstand view. He heard the gasping sob as the cross was thrust into the hole prepared for it. But still the Man neither complained or moaned, but only prayed. Simon heard, and Simon's heart was broken, and Simon surrendered. Ever after he carried Christ's cross joyously. Its cruel hardness had pressed against his back. But One had died for him. He sensed the grand and glorious truth that when he bore the cross the Other would die for him! So long as he believed, the Other would bleed. And Simon learned to believe with all his heart.

I like to think that Simon stood there by the cross, alone even in the midst of that mad crowd, absorbed for hours by the One whom he had helped. Then God turned out His light. Was this that His Son's final agony should be witnessed by none? Simon probably remained there in the darkness believing more and more fully as the hours went slowly by.

Have you ever wondered whether Jesus thanked Simon for bearing His cross? Do you think Simon expected thanks for his deed? I think not! He actually was grateful for the privilege! Grateful that he had been forced to carry the cross. Perhaps he remembered whispers of Christ's words quoted to him by his sons, "If any man will come after me, let him . . . take up his cross, and follow me." Simon never expected thanks; he gave thanks! As he looked back along the road over which God had led his feet he rejoiced. Everything had worked out so well in the end. The events of his life had come into focus.

There are some of us today who are thus dramatically confronted with the Crucified and His cross. We find ourselves where we are compelled to carry it! The cross is being thrust upon us against our wills. Like Simon, we too are "compelled" to carry out Christian acts. Let us carefully analyze our reactions. Do you fight the right because you want the wrong?

Perhaps your name is Simon—and you have to carry the cross. Then you hear a prayer, and you know you are part of that prayer. Nothing in life comes by blind chance. As you look back at today from the vantage point of tomorrow you will discern that God's providences have eyes "before and behind." No circumstance of your life is hidden from His scrutiny. The Spirit of God speaks to your heart and appeals to your mind and whispers in your soul. "This is the way, walk ye in it." Occasionally it may seem that you are actually being conscripted. Sometimes you may feel that you are being loaded with the cross against your desires. Remember Simon! Ever after he was grateful! He wanted no thanks. He requested no payment. The privilege was his entirely. Temporal and eternal benefits came with the burden he bore. For Simon, Old Skull Face no longer leered. It became the smile of God to his soul. It will for you, too, my friend.

The cross that was laid upon Simon is our cross. He made a contribution to the plan of our salvation like that made by no one since. Jesus might have said, "Wherever the gospel story is told, the story of Simon and the cross will be told also." Simon did not preach at Pentecost. We are not told that he went to the ends of the earth and established churches. In fact, we are not told that he did anything after Calvary. But this we know: He eased Christ's burden. He made our Lord's pain less by sharing His cross. He sets us a worthy example. Jesus tells us now, "If any man will come after me, let him ... take up his cross ..." Are you ready to do this?

I want you to look into your own heart now. Can you see there, with the light of the Spirit shining into your mind, anything that will destroy you if it is not destroyed? Does some hidden sin that you have not yet placed on the cross lurk in the darkness of your soul? Are you ready to give it to Jesus now? Can you see some task you ought to do but which you have postponed because the price is too great? Take it up today. He will satisfy your every longing. Do not delay. Pray, "Lord Jesus, here are my sins. Nail them to the cross. Give me power to do Thy will. I lay the consequences at Thy feet, and take Thy cross and follow Thee."

Chapter 2

Herod the Crafty

Edomite King—"That Fox"

The encounter of Herod with Jesus was a dramatic moment in history. Jesus, the lowly Nazarene and the representative of God's chosen people, was descended from Jacob. Herod, the proud and wily half Edomite, was a scion of the nations that had sprung from Esau. He might have enjoyed the privileges and blessings that came from the Abrahamic covenant. But like his ancestor Esau, he was a profane person. And the enmity that had existed between Esau and Jacob, and which had often flared up among their descendants during the intervening years, reached a new focus at our Lord's trial. Herod and Jesus confronted each other in the palace of the Edomite king. Here Herod's feelings against Jesus were clearly revealed.

The factors that made this encounter even more dramatic had begun some years previously. The father of this Herod had sought to destroy the baby Jesus. His plans had been frustrated by an angel of the Lord. The authority and jurisdiction of the father had been divided among several of his sons. The lives of the families of the Herods were dissolute and evil in the extreme. Murder and intrigue, disloyalty and impurity, characterized their conduct.

Herod Antipas was tetrarch of Galilee and Perea when John the Baptist preached. We know from the story of the Gospels how he had amorously snatched away the wife of his brother Philip. This woman, Herodias, cruel, wicked, scheming—the New Testament Jezebel—grew completely unscrupulous. Her first husband had lacked the ambition and flamboyance she thought necessary for the position for which she longed. So she tossed him aside for his brother.

When we are introduced to him in the Gospels, Herod Antipas was not altogether bad. He was greatly intrigued by the preaching of John the Baptist. Mark notes some remarkable facts in this connection. "Herod himself had sent forth and laid hold upon John, and bound him in prison for Herodias' sake, his brother Philip's wife: for he had married her. For John had said unto Herod, It is not lawful for thee to have thy brother's wife. Therefore Herodias had a quarrel against him, and would have killed him; but she could not" (Mark 6:17-19). Observe this further piece of information: "For Herod feared John, knowing that he was a just man and an holy, and observed him; and when he heard him, he did many things, and heard him gladly" (verse 20).

Herod had listened to John and valued his instruction. We are told that he "observed him," that is, he protected him. Herod saved John alive because he knew that Herodias was trying to encompass his death. So the best way out of the difficulty, Herod thought, was to bring John into house arrest and keep him safe. His personal guards would prevent the paid assassins of Herodias from getting at the Baptist.

But Herodias was so disturbed by John's censure against her adultery that she resolved to bring about the death of the Baptist by any means she might be able to devise. Her opportunity came at a birthday celebration organized by Herod. Herod's guests were his high captains and chief officers of Galilee. This would seem to make the occasion more a political feast than a family gathering. Wine flowed freely. As the feast progressed the blasé guests looked for more and more exciting entertainment.

It was then that Herodias sent her daughter, Salome, into the festal hall to dance. This act was out of the ordinary. The young girl, just entering womanhood, danced with abandon before the drunken company. His wits bemused with liquor, the besotted Herod made a foolish promise. Anything she wanted, even to the half of his kingdom, should be hers for the asking, he cried. No one says a thing like that when sober. And Herod was not! Salome immediately left the hall to consult her mother. "What shall I ask?" she must have queried excitedly. The dark suggestion shot back immediately. "The head of John the Baptist in a dish!" Did Salome quail? Did she demur? We do not know. That she returned to the banquet with her outrageous demand we are told. This immediately electrified the entire company.

Everyone was suddenly sober. This was no ordinary request, and Herod looked around the company of his friends for someone to take him off the hook. If anyone had said, "That's not a fair request for this kind of promise," Herod would have turned away from his dark deed. He longed to be spared from carrying out his promise. But he was too proud to renege. Here is a lesson we ought never to forget: Two wrongs never make a right. Always remember that. Sometimes we have to decide a question. So we take a vote or carry out an act. We discover later that we have made a mistake. Often, in order to cover this up, we decide to make another mistake! Never do this. The best time to correct an error is when you find out about it. If you tell a lie to get out of a problem you will find that this will not be the last one you will feel you need to tell! You will think that you must tell many more to cover up your tracks. Then you will get so tangled up you will eventually have to call it quits! Say, "Please forgive me! I want to start anew." But the best thing to do is not to begin telling lies in the first place.

Herod had made a foolish promise. He knew he had made a mistake that was terrible. He should have done something at once about correcting the situation while there was still opportunity to do so. When he asked Salome for suggestions for a gift, he was thinking of simple items. He promised only normal things, not that murder might be committed! Herod's friends did not want murder either, because they all respected John. Herod allowed pride to dominate his will. He was not ready to lose face and to say, "I spoke foolishly. I was half drunk. Let's start all over again." He was too much of a coward to say this. Herod's golden moment of decision came and went.

And so an executioner was sent to the Baptist's cell. Without warning, with no preparation for his end, John was put to death. His head was brought immediately into the banqueting hall. The revelry ended. The guests, shocked and sobered, must have gone back quietly to their rooms.

When Herodias saw those lips that had condemned her unlawful union now silent, she exulted. She had hoped that by leaving one husband and attaching herself to another she would attain her ambitions. She felt that John stood in her way. So she removed him and continued the upward thrust that her restless and relentless and cruel self-will directed.

The disciples of John came and took his mutilated body away and buried it. Hearing of this tragedy, Jesus said to His disciples, in effect, "Come, let us rest awhile. Let's think this thing through." Earlier He had organized and sent them out as evangelists, two and two. And they had gone everywhere preaching, healing, restoring, building.

And when Herod later heard of Christ, he thought that John the Baptist must have risen from the dead. He was terrified by this idea. No peace or happiness ever after came to the unfortunate king. He then set out to silence his accusing conscience by stilling Christ's voice. Some weeks later "there came certain of the Pharisees, saying unto him, Get thee out, and depart hence: for Herod will kill thee. And he said unto them, Go ye, and tell that fox, Behold, I cast out devils, and I do cures to day and to morrow, and the third day I shall be perfected. Nevertheless I must walk to day, and to morrow, and the day following: for it cannot be that a prophet perish out of Jerusalem" (Luke 13:31-33).

Near Newbold College, in England, are burrows in which foxes live. Going there to teach a few years ago, I discovered that the college was no longer raising chickens, although the farm once had done so. The reason for the change was the work of vixens! One had succeeded in entering the large pen. She evidently wanted a hen for her pups. In her lust for blood she killed every fowl in the run, scores and scores of them. So the farmer buried the piles of birds, cleaned up the place, and raised a new flock in what he thought was a foxproof shelter. A year or so later the crafty vixen repeated her performance! She needed only one hen for her family, but joy in needless killing and extreme craftiness characterize a vixen. Herod was a cunning killer. He derived some thrill from murder.

But Jesus, in effect, responded to his threats: "I have a job to do for today and tomorrow. And while it is still today and tomorrow I will carry out My tasks in spite of Herod. The third day My life will reach its consummation." I think that a reply like this must have sent cold shivers down Herod's spine. Here was a Man who was unafraid and who had a destiny to fulfill. He was ready to die when His life's purpose was achieved. He named Jerusalem as the place of the end!

So Christ's life ran swiftly to its culmination. At the crisis at its close Jesus was confronted by the Roman governor in the judgment hall. One of the moves Pilate made to shift responsibility was to send Him to Herod. The priests had associated Jesus with Galilee, and so Pilate rationalized his course of action (*The Desire of Ages*, p. 728).

On that Friday morning somebody knocked at Herod's palace gate, and suddenly the king was face to face with Jesus. "When Herod saw Jesus, he was exceeding glad: for he was desirous to see him of a long season, because he had heard many things of him; and he hoped to have seen some miracle done by him" (Luke 23:8).

Herod had the decrepit and maimed brought into his palace, and then he challenged Jesus to work a miracle, promising that he would let Him go (*ibid.*, p. 729). But Christ answered him nothing. This is a remarkable insight into God's methods with men. Herod had silenced the voice of the greatest of the prophets, John the Baptist. Because of the king's rejection of the truth, God's Son had nothing more to say to him. "Christ was as one who heard and saw not" (*ibid.*). That is the way of life. When we turn a deaf ear to the invitation of Christ through His messengers, no miracle will be worked for us. No spectacular demonstrations of divine power and divine grace will be carried out to deepen our faith. Jesus "answered him nothing."

The chief priests and the scribes stood by and vehemently accused Him. Then "Herod with his men of war set him at nought, and mocked him, and arrayed him in a gorgeous robe, and sent him again to Pilate" (Luke 23:11). Notice that it was Herod, frustrated in his efforts to induce Christ to perform a miracle, who egged on his men of war to mock and insult Jesus. So angry did the king become that he actually led his soldiers in heaping indignities upon the Savior. Christ was tossed about among Herod's soldiers, "dragged this way and that" (*ibid.*, p. 731).

Each rough man sought to pull Him limb from limb. Some struck Him as He passed them. Pilate's soldiers decided that they had better rescue the Prisoner, or He would be pulled to pieces. It was Herod who had the idea to array Jesus in a gorgeous robe.

There are several terms that we might use to describe this monarch, but none of them would be pleasant. Here are some from the pen of inspiration: "There is the haughty Herod who jeered at His royal title, and bade the mocking soldiers crown Him king" (*The Great Controversy,* p. 643). "The cowardly and cruel Herod" (*ibid.,* p. 667). "The dissolute king" (*The Desire of Ages,* p. 214). Haughty, cowardly, cruel, dissolute, what a catalog this is! The Savior had nothing to say to him. Christ performed no miracle to save Himself. Even such a one as Herod was afraid to put Him to death. He sensed that this Man of Nazareth was without guilt. So he sent Him back to Pilate.

For Herod the golden moment had passed forever. At the instigation of Herodias he later made application to the emperor, Caligula, for greater honors. But Agrippa, angry with him, sent a complaint to Rome. Herod was summoned to appear in person before Caesar. There he was stripped of all his honors and titles and powers and banished to either Gaul or Spain. The historian Josephus records the only good act of Herodias—she accompanied her husband into exile and took care of him. Somewhere, in unknown graves, this foolish and evil couple lie buried, their ambitions never realized.

We survey the story of this man with horror. His encounter with Christ reached its focus on the day of Calvary. We note the climax of his decision. He was haughty and ambitious, cruel, cowardly, and dissolute. Joining himself in a sinful alliance, because of the thrust of his passion, with an even more abandoned woman, he brooked no restraints. Carried away by his regard for her, sac-

rificing the life of the greatest of the prophets, Herod at last came
face to face with the Savior of humanity and then received no answer to his problems.

Sometime in that journey to doom he had heard God's servant John preach. He had listened to him. He had actually begun
to do many things the Baptist recommended. But he had not
committed his life to the Master. And at last all the ambition, all
the position, all the prestige, and all the lust for which he longed
and for which he was ready to sacrifice everything, even the lives
of good men, were stripped from him in the moment in which
he thought he had attained them. Finally, a foreigner in an alien
land, alone, poor, left to his memories, his life passed to its end. A
horrible picture! A completely needless result!

Herod was descended from Abraham. He might have shared
all the promised blessings. But he was like his ancestor Esau, a
man wrapped up in material things. He too was a "profane person" (Heb. 12:16). He too sold his birthright for a mess of pot-
tage, for a moment of pleasure, for an hour of adulation, and by
that sale destroyed himself.

As you look over the entire life of this man, where would
you say he took that first fatal step in the wrong direction? He
might have been recorded in the book of history as the king who
had rescued Jesus. He could have grown famous as the one who
had pledged himself to defend innocent men. But this was not to
be. He did not realize that his destiny depended on his aligning
himself with Christ's prophet and with Christ's program. He
thought he could gain his own goals by cutting right across the
principles and purposes and policies of the Man of Galilee. But
in that decision he destroyed himself.

As we look back over his journey into oblivion, we note that
when he turned his back on the messages of God's prophet he

turned his back on Heaven. He did not sense it at the time. That point of no return came with no blare of trumpets. It arrived during a dinner party, with the plates of gold and silver and rare goblets before him, with the rustle of silk dresses and the fragrance of women's perfume and the glamour of the midnight hour. The point of decision, the needlepoint, had been reached, but he knew it not. He debated back and forth when he realized the implications of his oath, and then decided to plunge into the abyss. And the light went out for Herod.

The great decisions of life do not announce themselves. This big moment steals upon us as stealthily as the midnight thief, and the moment of deciding is the unexpected moment. But with this there is another point of vital importance. It is not by our isolated acts, either good or evil, that the character is decided for heaven or hell, but by the general tendency of our lives. By little decisions Herod turned his life into the riptide that flowed in the direction of self, pride, love of power, position, social prestige, royal titles, life in high places, earthly honor, and lust. That program grew like a tidal wave, driven by a gale, until it carried everything before it, even all thought of righteousness and eternity. His is a solemn story, a sad story, a warning and an instruction. Confronted with Calvary, he crucified the Son of God, put Him to open shame and sent Him to the tomb, and went back to business.

May the Lord open our eyes to see where lies the tendency of our lives. When the crisis comes it will be too late to prepare. Fix your mind on things above, and the power of Omnipotence will support you.

Chapter 3

Caiaphas the Cynical

High Priest—"It Is Expedient"

In the trial and condemnation of Christ, Caiaphas the cunning played a major role. His position as the high priest enabled him to dominate the opinions of his contemporaries. With his father-in-law, Annas, Caiaphas manipulated the ideas and purposes of the other members of the Sanhedrin.

A quarter of a century before the ministry of our Lord, Annas the Sadducee was appointed to the office of high priest. Israel had sunk so far in degradation that the position of high priest was designated by the Roman governor. The sacred and hereditary office, by command of God open only to the first-born descendant of Aaron, was now a gift of politicians and a sinecure of unscrupulous and ambitious men. Soon deposed, Annas was followed in office by five of his sons and his son-in-law Caiaphas.

That a Sadducee should hold this office is all but incredible. Believing neither in angel nor in spirit, refusing to acknowledge that at last he would be arraigned before the Eternal judge, denying the existence of any hope for the hereafter, the Sadducee was the cynical materialist of his day. Only a hypocrite could remain a Sadducee and function as a high priest. Annas and Caiaphas were such hypocrites. Among their "family connections were Sadducees, proud, bold, reckless, full of ambition and cruelty, which they hid under a cloak of pretended righteousness" (*The Desire of Ages*, p. 539). They filled the office, not for what they could put into it, but only for what they could extract from it.

After his deposition from the office of high priest, Annas had played his hand behind the scenes. His power was as great a score of years later. For this reason his name is mentioned with his son-in-law in the Gospel story (Luke 3:2). Both men are called high priest. Further indication of his prestige is given by the fact that Jesus was taken first to Annas after He had been arrested. "His artifice, cunning, and subtlety must be used on this occasion" (*ibid.*, p. 698).

After His encounter with the older high priest, Christ was dragged before Caiaphas (John 18:24). Caiaphas is called the high priest "that same year" (verse 13).

Caiaphas, a member of Annas' family and a Sadducee, was the most powerful Jew of his day. With little regard for theoretical ideas of morality or theological concepts of sin, he sought to gain all he could from the present. Cynical magistrate, hypocritical high priest, unscrupulous ruler that he was, he worked only for his own advantages. His term of office spanned Christ's ministry.

Christ was brought for trial before this man. We first encounter Caiaphas in a scene in the Sanhedrin. The meeting had been called because of the resurrection of Lazarus. This miracle had been witnessed by many who were ready to swear, beyond any argument, that they had seen him dead and watched him come to life at the command of Christ. Because of this miracle the claims of Jesus to be the Messiah were becoming more firmly established each day. The position of the ruling hierarchy of the Jews, on the contrary, was becoming more precarious in proportion. The Sanhedrin had taken its stand against Jesus. Should the people acknowledge Him as the Messiah, the prestige of the highest Hebrew legislative authority would be in jeopardy. The pseudoscientific position of the Sadducees, now invalidated by a genuine resurrection, was shaken to the core. John summarized the quandary of these men thus: "Then gathered the chief priests and the Pharisees a council, and said, What do we? for this man doeth many miracles. If we let him thus alone, all men will believe on him: and the Romans shall come and take away both our place and nation. And one of them, named Caiaphas, being the high priest that same year, said unto them, Ye know nothing at all, nor consider that it is expedient for us, that one man should die for the people, and that the whole nation perish not. And this spake he not of himself: but being high priest that year, he prophesied that Jesus should die for that nation; and not for the nation only, but that also he should gather together in one the children of God that were scattered abroad. Then from that day forth they took counsel together for to put him to death" (John 11:47-53). "How blindly did the haughty Caiaphas acknowledge the Savior's mission! . . . Among the heathen, the dim consciousness that one was to die for the human race had led to the offering of human sacrifices. So Caiaphas proposed by the sacrifice of Jesus to save the guilty nation, not from transgression, but in transgression, that they might continue in sin" (*ibid.*, p. 540).

Caiaphas emerges from this scene as "a proud and cruel man, overbearing and intolerant" (*ibid.*, p. 539). He was cynical, relentless, politic, arrogant and domineering. To address his peers with the phrase "Ye know nothing at all" (John 11:49) reveals his self-assurance and sense of power. He had little respect for gray heads. He was completely certain of his position and afraid of nothing.

The next window into his character is provided by his phrase "It is expedient" (John 11:50). Here speaks the politic man. What is expedient is right! The advantage of the moment must be purchased at any price! But Caiaphas was not finished with his self-revelation. "That one man should die for the people, and that the whole nation perish not" (verse 50). Human life meant little to Caiaphas! If the only way out of their quandary was the murder of Jesus of Nazareth, why not take it? Here is the cynic speaking! Remove whoever stands in the way and don't give that person another thought! And so the plot was laid. Jesus must be taken out of the way at all cost and by any suitable method. The bribery of Judas, the betrayal of Christ, the Sanhedrin called into an illegal session at an unlawful hour, with responsible members deliberately excluded—all these were the results of this policy instigated by Caiaphas.

When face to face with the despairing Judas, Caiaphas showed his cynical trait even more clearly. Before the Sanhedrin Judas burst in with the cry "I have betrayed the innocent blood." "What is that to us?" Caiaphas retorted contemptuously. "See thou to that" (Matt. 27:4; cf. *The Desire of Ages*, p. 722). With a curl of his lips he dismissed Judas. He had paid him the bargained price. That was the end of the matter!

Now we see Jesus face to face with Caiaphas (John 18: 13, 14, 24-28; Matt. 26:57-68; Mark 14:53-65; Luke 22: 54-65). The wily high priest is shown at his worst in this encounter. Let us note carefully his twisted policies. He sought for false witnesses to invent charges against Jesus to put Him to death (Matt. 26:59-61). Even *he* at first failed to find any! He tried to taunt Christ into making a statement that might be turned against Him (verse 62; Mark 14:60). He then put Christ under judicial oath to declare His position. Caiaphas demanded to know, Was He, or was He not, the Messiah (Matt. 26:63; Mark 14:61)? To this Jesus gave the judicial affirmation. Then He foretold that Caiaphas would one day witness the glorious Second Advent. "The words of Christ startled the high priest. . . . There rushed before his mind as a panorama the scenes of the final judgment. For a moment he saw the fearful spectacle of the graves giving up their dead, with the secrets he had hoped were forever hidden. For a moment he felt as if standing before the eternal judge, whose eye, which sees all things, was reading his soul, bringing to light mysteries supposed to be hidden with the dead.

"The scene passed from the priest's vision. Christ's words cut him, the Sadducee, to the quick" (*The Desire* of Ages, p. 708). The high priest then showed his complete disregard of the law: he tore his official garments in two (Matt. 26:65; Mark 14:63). "Conviction mingled with passion led Caiaphas to do as he did. He was furious with himself for believing Christ's words" (*ibid.*). Here was his golden moment. But he brushed it aside. He next condemned Jesus upon His own testimony. This, too, was illegal. He permitted his followers to ridicule and mistreat the Prisoner (Matt. 26:67, 68; Mark 14:65), actions also forbidden by the law. "Never was criminal treated in so inhuman a manner as was the Son of God" (*ibid.*, p. 710). And all this took place in the court of Caiaphas!

Caiaphas appears in an equally bad light when he argues the case against Christ before Pilate; he was probably the main prosecutor before the governor (Matt. 27:12). When asked by Pilate what the charge was, the Jews evidently detected disdain in the Roman's tone. Their response shows they were not afraid of the governor. "If he were not a malefactor, we would not have delivered him up unto thee" (John 18:30). To Pilate's retort "Take ye him and judge him according to your law," they responded tartly, "It is not lawful for us to put any man to death" (John 18: 31). Two unscrupulous men, the Hebrew high priest and the Roman magistrate, communicated perfectly in this dialog. As the web tightened about the hapless Pilate, the Jews became more and more daring. Again, it was probably Caiaphas who moved the rabble to demand Barabbas' release (Mark 15: 11; Matt. 27:20), who roused them to shout "Crucify," and who, on Calvary, led in the mocking jests directed against the dying Savior (Matt. 27:41–43). And when the sun set that Friday, Caiaphas must have felt he had gained his objectives. His enemy was dead, and in His dying had been greatly and satisfyingly humiliated. Such a man was Caiaphas the cynical.

The character of Caiaphas was finally revealed by the cross. Cold and calculating, callous, cruel, relentless schemer that he was, Caiaphas worked only to get his own way. The feelings of others, the eternal needs of his people and of all humanity, all these and more he was ready to brush aside that his present will might be carried out. He underlines the solemn truth that even in the highest religious positions men may degenerate into crass materialists living only for today. Proximity to sacred things does not of itself make someone holy. A sacred office may not give rise to sacred thoughts and a godly life. Let us beware lest we become indifferent to the sacred truths we believe and by our acts repudiate the Savior we claim to adore.

Chapter 4

Pilate the Cowardly

Roman Judge—"I Am Innocent"

Before the dawn of a Passover day nineteen hundred years ago, Pilate was rudely awakened. He dressed hurriedly and made his way to his now-familiar seat of judgment. The Paschal season being in progress, the Hebrew leaders refused to enter his chamber lest they be defiled. Perhaps he was irritated, but Pilate had learned to live with the Jews. He probably had the governor's chair brought up onto the porch as a concession to them. Before him milled the chief priests, scribes, and rulers. They held the Prisoner in their midst. Pilate knew these citizens as well as they knew him! There was little love lost between them.

Pilate, tradition holds, was a soldier of fortune. Growing up in army camps, he took to the sword, resolving to make his career in fighting. His bravery and dedication to war attracted the attention of Caesar. When asked what reward he wished, Pilate volunteered for the post of governor of Judea. He well knew that if he failed in this position his career would end. But should he succeed in maintaining the *lex et pax Romana* in this most difficult of provinces, there was very little that his ambition might not achieve.

This Friday morning Pilate found himself, as representative of Caesar, on Caesar's judgment seat. The Roman soldiers stood ready to enforce his decisions. He now faced the Prisoner, about whom he had likely heard a great deal. Everyone in Judea knew of Jesus. There were blind who could see because of Him. Those born lame or deaf He had restored. There were even some who had died, to whom He had spoken life. Entire villages through which He had passed could list not one sick person. The name of Jesus of Nazareth was on every tongue. Pilate's soldiers must have made careful notes of all He said and did. At first Pilate had been fearful of taking action lest He should stir up a revolution against Rome. This Nazarene must be watched! But eventually the governor must have reached half-formed opinions that His nature, His teaching, His works, His very presence, undermined all suspicion.

And now, apparently for the first time, Pilate is face to face with Jesus. Enemies were about the Prisoner like baying wolves. These accusers were seeking every pretext to destroy Him. Haughty, disdainful, cynical, Pilate queried, "What accusation bring you against Him?" The Roman's very tone must have told the Jews that he did not believe that any just accusation could be made to stand up in law. The priests snapped back in effect, "Had He not been guilty, we would not have brought Him here. He claims to be king!" Pilate turned to Jesus and asked, "Art thou the king of the Jews?" To which Jesus replied, "Thou sayest" (Matt. 27:11).

Something about Jesus' voice, His appearance, His manner, and His authority must have impressed Pilate. He took the Nazarene out to a private chamber and there talked to Him about the kingdom of truth. In that discussion the governor was greatly impressed. Christ, in turn, asked him questions. In response to one of Pilate's, Jesus questioned in effect, "Are you asking this because you have a sincere desire to know, or did somebody put ideas into your mind about My work and about My kingdom?" Pilate's pride was stung. "Your own people do not believe You," he retorted. "How can you expect me to believe? Do you know that I could either destroy You or let You go?" The Nazarene responded gently, "You can do nothing to Me except it be given you from above." Mystified, Pilate asked, "Are You a king? Why are You here?" And Christ responded, "My kingdom is not of this world. If it were, My servants would fight." "What is Your kingdom?" the governor now bantered. "I have come to bear witness of truth," Jesus affirmed solemnly. "What is truth?" Pilate inquired. He had dealt with persons to whom truth was a foreign currency. Realizing that in Jesus was a being far beyond his comprehension, Pilate went back to the judgment seat and strove diligently to release the Prisoner. But the leaders of the people would have nothing to do with his plan. In his frustration Pilate reached an impasse. All the while the Prisoner stood silent before him.

In response to a prayer of Christ (*The Desire of Ages,* p. 732), an angel had been sent from heaven. In a dream Pilate's wife witnessed this very judgment scene. She looked beyond it, far into the future, and watched Jesus Christ, as King of kings and Lord of lords, return to this earth in glory. She saw that the Judge, the Omnipotent, was about to be condemned by her husband! Horror filled her heart. Quickly she scribbled a note. A messenger hurried in before the governor with it. Pilate read with foreboding his wife's experience. Exactly what he thought we shall never know. But he strove all the more to free the Prisoner.

At this juncture Pilate made his first fatal blunder. "Let me scourge Him," he suggested, "and let Him go." The governor had already declared that he found no fault with Him. But he felt that the sight of a little blood and a little torture might satisfy the priests! The Roman flagellation could bring a man to the threshold of death. Many actually died under this torture. Leather thongs, to which pieces of metal or bones were affixed, were attached to a handle. This instrument was used to lash the unfortunate victim. The prisoner was bound over a central shaft. The *tortor* might wrap the scourges around his stomach. If he wished, he could completely disembowel him. Sometimes this happened. It was part of the responsibility of the governor to stop this beating before it ended in tragedy.

And those who wished Jesus dead gloated while He was scourged. No word escaped His lips. No condemnation of His enemies and no criticism of this miscarriage of justice were spoken by the Son of God. When it was over, the cords that bound Him to the pillar were cut. Jesus probably fell unconscious to the ground. Revived, He would again be forced to stand trembling before the governor.

Pilate had observed many men in similar plight. He had seen them suffering. He had watched them under accusation. He could read criminal human nature like a book. Never had he seen one such as this. And he strove the more to let Him go.

Pilate had sent Jesus to Herod in a vain attempt to shift responsibility, but now the decision was back on himself. Then a new thought struck the governor. At the Paschal season it was customary for one political prisoner to be granted amnesty. Pilate hoped for two objects when he declared, "I will let Jesus go free." He planned to release the prisoner because of the Hebrews and also to spare the innocent One. But the Jewish leaders would have nothing to do with his offer. Then Pilate thought of his worst case, Barabbas, condemned for both sedition and murder. He felt that should he place the two together Jesus would surely be the people's choice. But the cry "Barabbas!" shattered his hopes! How could they choose a murderer and rebel in place of the Life-giver and Preacher of righteousness? But they clamored for Barabbas and would crucify Jesus. "Crucify! Crucify!" The horrible chant continued until reason and justice were driven from Pilate's mind.

The two prisoners were very opposite in character. One was a murderer, the other the Life-giver. One was a rebel, the other the Lawmaker. One was a traitor, the other the King of the universe. One was a sinner, the other the Sacrifice for sins. There they stood together. Pilate was so disgusted with the people's choice of Barabbas that he cried, "Bring me a basin." He hoped to wash away his responsibilities by a symbolic act. He tried to shift to the scribes and Pharisees the blame for his weakness. What he actually did was to condemn himself. Pilate chose Barabbas too. What strange thoughts must have chased one another in Pilate's mind as he went to breakfast!

The governor had been entrusted with the power of life and death. He could have freed the innocent One had he been strong. But earlier in the trial he had shown weakness. Now he could not face the thrust of the Jews: "This man claims to be king. Any man who claims to be a king is not Caesar's friend." Pilate had ever felt that his future depended on his friendship with Caesar. And now his political position, his ambition, all his life's schemes, seemed to hinge on what he would do with an innocent Man. He ordered Jesus to be scourged a second time. Then, buffeted by the Roman soldiers, blindfolded, a reed for a scepter thrust between His trembling fingers, struck on the face, Christ stood forth in all His humble majesty. Every man in the ugly assembly knew that He was innocent. Pilate was certain that his Prisoner was guiltless. Yet the governor nodded to a soldier. The cross was brought, and Jesus was taken out to the place of execution. It was at Pilate's order that the title was placed on the cross noting the "crime" of the Crucified. He had it written in three languages that all might read—Greek, Hebrew, and Latin. Each noted that Jesus had laid claim to be king.

Pilate could have stopped this mockery at any moment. But

because he felt that his ambition might not be realized if he did, that his coveted position might be lost, he allowed circumstances to take control of his better judgment.

A few years after the crucifixion Pilate was removed from office. He had made many foolish mistakes during his administration in Palestine. He had gone out of his way to irritate and snub and humiliate the Jewish leaders. The Galileans gave him trouble, and when a band of pious Galileans came down to Jerusalem he sent a contingent of his men into the Temple to mingle their blood with the blood of the sacrifices they were offering. After several of these stupid acts of unnecessary cruelty, the Samaritans complained against Pilate. He was summoned to Rome, but before he arrived the emperor, Tiberius, died. He was stripped of his honors and relieved of his position. Exiled and broken, according to tradition he committed suicide.

In Pilate we see one who watched God executed. He placed against eternal truth and eternal righteousness the ambitions of the passing moment. Pilate put his friendship with Caesar uppermost in his life and crucified the Son of God. The future he squandered for the now. Its transient honors, its fading glories, its transitory privileges, he bought with the denial of truth, the flinging aside of justice, with cruelty and useless mockery of right. In making this choice he squandered everything. He lost his wealth, his power, and his position. Broken, humiliated, drunken, with his peace of mind gone forever, he died by his own hand.

Jesus is crucified before us whenever we choose to think about it. In our hearts, as we hear this story, we can travel back to the Place of the Skull. In imagination we may watch Jesus lifted up between heaven and earth. We can see Him bearing our sins in His own body on the tree. We can love Him in appreciation, or we can forget Him in indifference. We can accept Him as our

Savior, yield to Him in affectionate obedience, or we can brush Him aside.

The question that Pilate asked, "What shall I do then with Jesus which is called Christ?" is one we all must ask ourselves. What are you going to do with Him? Is He your Savior, or is He just a name? Is He the one altogether lovely, or is He one whom you associate with a narrow way of life? Does He stand in the way of your friendship with any person? Does His will cut across the path you tread toward some cherished position? If any of these questions apply to you, you are where Pilate was nineteen hundred years ago. The Roman thought that by pushing Jesus aside he could keep his friends. He hoped that by removing the Nazarene he could retain his position. He decided that by giving Jesus up to the cruelty and ridicule of the mob he could better reach for worldly honors and privileges. But in grabbing what he thought was best in life, Pilate actually caught self-destruction. That result always follows such a choice.

Sometimes we wonder how those who once started on the right road can forget the precious experiences of their lives. How can they put God from their memories and thoughts? How can they dismiss as unnecessary what they know they ought to do? But once we settle on a course of wrongdoing, the right has gone out of our thinking. There is no limit, in this case, to the lengths in sin we may go. Pilate is an illustration of this tragedy. If we start on the downward path, the end is the abyss—unless we stop and find our way back to truth and right.

Today we each have Pilate's choice. Either we surrender to Jesus as our king, or we destroy Him and so eventually destroy ourselves. "What shall I do then with Jesus?" must be decided on our knees by each of us. Say to Him, "King of my soul, I crown Thee now."

Chapter 5

Nicodemus the Cautious

Teacher of Israel—"How?"

The person whom we now consider was, very likely, not actually present among the crowds at the Crucifixion. He was, nevertheless, dramatically connected with it and affected by it. In the same sense, although we were not actually there in Pilate's judgment hall or on Calvary, we are, for time and eternity, deeply affected by our relationship to Him who was there judged and put to death.

We always associate Nicodemus with Christ's teaching regarding the new birth. He is introduced to us by John. The narrative of Nicodemus' experience with Jesus is found in the third chapter of John's Gospel. There are words in this story that are of the greatest significance. Let us study them carefully.

Nicodemus was a Pharisee. This is a fact of the first importance. The Pharisees were a sect of the Jews. Today we despise Pharisees. I don't think we ought to scorn all of them with quite as much spleen as we do! They were very particular persons, and had the highest standards of conduct of any group in Israel. They carefully studied the minutiae of the law, and observed those details with constant care. They were separatists, having nothing to do with sin and its defilement, as they conceived them. Now, I know that many of the Pharisees did not live up to all these principles. Most of them, according to the judgment of our Lord, were hypocrites. But I don't think we should apply this term to Nicodemus. He was no hypocrite. He did his best to live according to all the standards he considered right. I don't believe we should apply this epithet of derogation to Saul of Tarsus, either. The last thing of which we could justly accuse either man is insincerity. So not all the Pharisees were as bad as one might be led to believe from the connotation of the term today.

Nicodemus was a man of the highest ideals, the loftiest standards, and the strongest discipline. In fact, we might almost call him meticulous in his adherence to his code of conduct. In his system of ethics and his determination to attain to the righteousness of the law he exhibited a resolution measured by all the powers of his will.

Nicodemus was also a "ruler of the Jews." The expression means that he was a member of the Hebrew senate, the Sanhedrin. This body was made up of persons of experience. These men were required to be fathers of families. It was hoped that they had developed understanding of the viewpoints of their rebellious or wayward sons. They possessed a certain measure of maturity from having lived long enough and having met often enough the vicissitudes of life. Among this group were men of ripe wisdom and rich experiences.

Nicodemus had the confidence of most of his contemporaries. His peers, and even those of the younger generation, recognized in him traits worthy of this high honor. And so this Pharisee found himself a member of the Sanhedrin, the highest judicial and governmental group among the Hebrew people.

In his conversation with Nicodemus, Jesus called attention to an important point concerning Nicodemus. He queried, "Art thou a master in Israel?" (John 3:10). The force of the Greek in this passage is "Are you that famous teacher in Israel?" Nicodemus was a highly respected theological teacher of Israel. This points up a very interesting characteristic. He had devoted himself to scriptural studies, and had worked on methods of clarifying his expositions. He had devised his techniques of relaying his knowledge and had attained a position as the revered and beloved teacher of God's chosen people. Nicodemus had reached an intellectual, theological, and judicial preeminence among his people.

"The same came to Jesus by night" (John 3:2). This piece of information opens a window into the disposition of Nicodemus. He was cautious. He moved slowly and with care. He was not yet ready to give himself fully to the cause of Christ. There are those who refuse to commit themselves immediately to some point. These diffident ones may be far wiser in their attitude than those who rush ahead. We may recall the sage remarks of Gamaliel, suggesting caution, made in a later sitting of the Sanhedrin. There were present in the assembly some firebrands who were ready to destroy Peter, James, John, and the other disciples. Gamaliel said, in effect, "Truth is its own vindicator. Leave these men alone. If it is God who is backing the Christianity they are propagating, we fight the impossible. If it is the devil, it contains the seeds of its own destruction" (see Acts 5:34-39). These are sober and good words.

Nicodemus sought Jesus out. He found by inquiry where He would likely be. Perhaps they met under the olive trees on Olivet. The city was hushed in slumber. But with pounding heart and strange feelings of timidity Nicodemus discussed the problem that was troubling him (*The Desire of Ages,* p. 168).

Nicodemus came to Christ with compliments. The Savior listened to him politely. Then He made a startling declaration, "Except a man be born again, he cannot see the kingdom of God" (John 3:3). Nicodemus met this with what he must have regarded as irrefutable logic. This "birth" was obviously physically

absurd. How can a grown person be born again? he queried iron-
ically. A human being is the product of all the experiences un-
dergone from infancy. It is surely just as impossible to begin again
intellectually and spiritually as it is to revert into an embryo physically, his answer suggested. But Jesus never sought to refute logic
with logic. The Savior persuaded by declaration and illustration.

The evening breezes stirred the trees and sighed in the
branches. "Listen, Nicodemus," He whispered in effect. "Hear the
wind! It comes, it goes! We know it only by its murmuring move-
ments. It is so with the workings of the Spirit." And then the
Lord turned the biblical scholar to a biblical illustration. "As
Moses lifted up the serpent in the wilderness, even so must the
Son of man be lifted up" (John 3:14). Have you ever wondered
how merely looking at a bronze snake could heal a man dying of
snakebite? Faith is the answer. Faith in God's plan. There is no
"scientific" reason. Faith is beyond reason. But it can be demonstrated in the life. The cured Israelites could testify that faith in
God's method worked. Illumination, like a brilliant searchlight,
revealed to the rabbi's mind the relevant truths of Scripture in
their proper relationships. In a flash the statements of Christ
seemed to fit into a perfect pattern. Passages from the inspired
page, which he knew so well, were joined to other passages. The
mosaic of truth formed a path to its goal in added and clearer
perceptions of truth. Predictions in the Old Testament pointed
to their consummation in the death of the Messiah for the sins of
humanity. Nicodemus knew he had been impelled by the Spirit.
He had felt a mysterious force drawing him as he had gone out
to meet Jesus. The pattern of Nicodemus' life was beginning to
shape up. The teacher of Israel left to ponder deeply.

Nicodemus was seemingly satisfied. He now rapidly came to
know for a fact that the Teacher sent from God was the Messiah.

He came to accept Christ's claim that He was the fulfillment of the antitype that centuries before had been lifted up in the wilderness so that the dying might look and live. Faith in the up-lifted serpent of bronze was the antidote to the venom of the serpent of death. And so He who knew no sin was the medicine for the poison of sin. He who was without the curse became cursed, that the cursed might live. God was among human beings and yet unrecognized by them. Nicodemus had not recognized Him before, but ultimately came to believe fully.

I can imagine that Nicodemus would seek out his most trusted friend, Joseph of Arimathea, who was also a member of the Sanhedrin. As they talked together, these rulers and biblical scholars, their convictions regarding the identity of Jesus of Nazareth must have deepened into a certainty. He was indeed the Christ. But they were both cautious men, too cautious. The months passed, and Nicodemus did not publicly take his stand for Him whom he knew to be the Messiah of the new kingdom.

Then, one day, Jesus was nailed to the cross. And before they realized fully what was happening, Jesus was dead on the cross. Then Nicodemus was certain that the prophecies had been carried out to the letter. Christ's own predictions of Himself had been fulfilled precisely. He had died on the cross and He was drawing men to Himself, just as He had said. These two men, Joseph and Nicodemus, sensed this to be a fact. They felt the drawing themselves. And so to Calvary they came that Friday afternoon and saw the need. So they called on Pilate and returned to the cross for the lifeless form of Christ. Nicodemus had 100 pounds of precious spikenard for the burying, and Joseph had a brand-new and empty tomb for the body. They were among the wealthiest, wisest, most respected men in the Holy City. Watch them tenderly take Jesus from the cross as they draw the nails from His stilled hands and feet. Those hands had worked only for humanity's needs and those feet had walked only on God's errands. They wrapped Him in the finest linen and laid Him lovingly to rest. Then Jesus was left by His weeping, helpful, but too cautious friends.

As we think of Nicodemus' response to truth and revelation, let us look behind his story to Christ's providential dealings with him. We have said all sorts of things about Nicodemus. He was too cautious, he was afraid to be counted. We might say many more things that would be partly true. But had we been there, we might well have done as he did. However, let us look carefully at Christ's dealings with this man. We watch His patience, His complete and practical understanding of the mind of the Hebrew rabbi. Jesus spoke few words of rebuke to this Pharisee because of his failure to grasp the symbolism of the Scriptures he professed to teach. He did not rail against him for not comprehending the vital doctrine of the new birth, but met him where he was. Christ saw, with His divine insight, the precise nature of this ruler's problem, and pointed to the very remedy needed. Then He allowed time for the Spirit to bring about the necessary changes in the attitude of Nicodemus. Jesus did not dog his heels or continue to knock at his door. He told him the truth, and then He prayed that the truth might bring about results in a transformed life.

The encounter with Nicodemus early in Christ's ministry brought forth results at its end. The deciding factor in the ruler's life was the cross. Through the cross light finally dawned in all its clarity. Through the cross light will always dawn in sincere hearts. Christ was lifted up, and the great Magnet of eternity began to pull at men's hearts. Is it drawing your heart today? Among the faceless ones about Golgotha are the overly cautious. Can you see yourself in the scared looks of those who hold back?

Christ has been patient with us. He does not rail upon us for our pharisaism or failure to live and teach what we pretend to know. He looks over the span of our lives, and when He sees that we possess the readiness to learn, He reveals His truth to our minds. As we contemplate the story, and its significance floods our lives, what are we going to do? Jesus says to us also, "You must be born again." The new birth will open our eyes to the full possibilities of the kingdom of God. Christ is ready to become the supreme ruler in our souls. The baptism of water and the Spirit will ensure our entry into His kingdom. The One who was sinless took our place so that we might look and trust and be drawn to Him and, taking His life, live it too. Every day we must do this. Every day we must die to our whims and ways and begin again. Every day we must conform our lives with His. Let us begin now.

Chapter 6

Peter the Craven

Chosen Disciple—"I Know Him Not"

Simon Peter is mentioned the most frequently of all the disciples in the Gospels. His position among the group of Christ's disciples was one of prominence. I believe that the veneration accorded him by some is wrong. But I feel that the comparative neglect or merely timid appraisal granted him by others is equally unjustifiable.

Peter was the leader among the disciples. He was the main spokesman of the apostolic band, even though his tongue ran away with him at times! His work in establishing the first Christian church, on human levels, is second only to that of Paul. He became a leader because by temperament he could lead. He would have led any group by the sheer force of his personality. Right or wrong, he could muster a crowd. He would then dilate at length on any subject, even though on occasion it might be said of him, as was the case at the Transfiguration, that he did not know what he was talking about (Luke 9:33). Let us try to form an idea of the kind of man he was from the evidence given in the inspired narratives.

I imagine Peter was a big, broad-shouldered man, with a smile that was wide and came easily, and a jaw set in resolution. Peter's father was named Jonah, or John (Matt. 16:17). His hometown was Bethsaida (John 1:44), on the shores of Galilee. Later Peter moved to the larger mercantile and fishing center of Capernaum. Here he lived in his own house with his wife and her mother, and probably also his brother Andrew. Peter owned his own boat (Luke 5:3). By any standard he was a successful and fairly prosperous fisherman.

In whatever part of the world they may be found, fishers are a breed apart. Much of their time is spent alone, very close to nature. They must be ready for all emergencies. Especially on Galilee's lake, 600 feet below sea level, conditions were often uncertain. The heat of the day caused an area of low pressure over the lake at sunset. Down the many valleys surrounding the water, the wind would rush. At times it reached the violence of gales, all the more dangerous because of coming so suddenly. The fishers who knew their waters would be ready for any eventualities. They must be brave and strong and active and self-reliant. Such a man was Simon Peter of Capernaum.

Simon, as boss of his little crew, was evidently used to getting his own way. This attitude spilled over into other relationships. Jesus observed, on one occasion toward the end of His ministry, "When thou wast young, thou girdedst thyself, and walkedst whither thou wouldest" (John 21:18).

We note this indication even in his relationship with Jesus, his master. A case in point was the time Peter actually rebuked Jesus for His submission to the circumstances that were leading Him to the cross (Matt. 16:22). Another occurred in the upper room when he flatly refused to permit God's Son to wash his feet (John 13:8). These are outstanding examples in which we see a mind unused to submitting readily to any will higher than its own.

Simon was impulsive. He was eager to try anything once. Nothing daunted him. On the storm-tossed sea he was ready to walk as Jesus walked (Matt. 14:28–31). Then there was the time after the second miraculous catch of fish, when, impatient at the slow progress of his boat, he plunged into the sea to swim ahead of it to meet his Lord in the dawn (John 21:7). He arrived only a few moments earlier than the others (verse 8).

Simon was a man of contradictions. One day he protested that Jesus was the Son of God, and on another he denied Him with oaths (Matt. 26:69-75). "Lord, not my feet only, but also my hands and my head" immediately followed an equally emphatic "Thou shalt never wash my feet" (John 13:8, 9). And Peter was what he was because of his heart. It was big and warm and loving. There was nothing mean about it, as there was nothing petty in what he did or said. He used superlatives (Luke 5:1-11; Matt. 19:27). He thought superlatively. With him it was all or nothing. Christ knew this. He set the pace for the other disciples.

Simon was also a deeply religious man. Sin weighed heavily upon him. He was conscious of its blight, and the crying need to have it removed. Because of this he listened eagerly to the ascetic preacher by the Jordan who was different from the ordinary run of rabbinic teachers. When Andrew later burst in upon him with the startling news of a "greater than John the Baptist," Simon was ready to respond to this further challenge to righteousness.

"He hastened to the Savior. The eye of Christ rested upon him, reading his character and his life history. His impulsive nature, his loving, sympathetic heart, his ambition and self-confidence, the history of his fall, his repentance, his labors, and his martyr death—the Savior read it all, and He said, 'Thou art Simon the son of Jona: thou shalt be called Cephas, which is by interpretation, A stone'" (*The Desire of Ages,* p. 139). Here may be found an analysis of Peter's motives.

On one occasion Jesus said to him, "Launch out into the deep, and let down your nets for a draught. And Simon answering said unto him, Master, we have toiled all the night, and have taken nothing: nevertheless at thy word I will let down the net. And when they had this done, they inclosed a great multitude of fishes: and their net brake. . . . When Simon Peter saw it, he fell down at Jesus' knees, saying, Depart from me; for I am a sinful man, O Lord. . . . And Jesus said unto Simon, Fear not; from henceforth thou shalt catch men. And when they had brought their ships to land, they forsook all, and followed him" (Luke 5:4-11).

Simon always had this vivid sense of his own sinfulness. His need was one of the ties that held him close to his Savior. There was no one else to whom he could go for the help and power he needed (John 6:68).

But Simon had a long and hard road to travel before he became the worker his Master designed him to be. "Peter was prompt and zealous in action, bold and uncompromising; and Christ saw in him material that would be of great value to the church. . . . These two men [Peter and Judas] represent the two classes that Christ connects with Himself, giving to them the advantages of His lessons and the example of His unselfish, compassionate life, that they may learn of Him" (*Testimonies,* vol. 4, p. 488).

Jesus gave those patient years of instruction to this disciple so that when he was converted he might strengthen his brethren (Luke 22:32). Every episode in Peter's experience Jesus used to teach him a lesson and mold his character. Peter walked on the water. He risked all. He exercised faith. The others sat in the ship and were too scared. They risked nothing. But it was Peter who sank.

Have you wondered why he sank? I imagine that he pictured his story on the front page of the local paper. He heard his own voice telling his grandson that grandpa had actually walked on the sea! His vanity blinded his vision of Jesus.

Peter was too self-confident. Jesus permitted him to pass through these experiences. This was to teach him that amid the storms of life, only connection with the Savior will prevent disaster. How much pain Peter might have saved himself if only he had learned this lesson by heart!

The crisis in the life of this apostle occurred on the night of the betrayal. Bold and impulsive as usual, he who had fled with the others at the arrest, having brandished his sword blindly, was now in the very palace of the high priest!

But before that fire, by the pillar of the court, Peter failed to realize that he had arrived at the most crucial point in his life. How like a thief such experiences come! One of the serving maids "had noticed that he came in with John, she marked the look of dejection on his face, and thought that he might be a disciple of Jesus. She was one of the servants of Caiaphas' household, and was curious to know. She said to Peter, 'Art not thou also one of this Man's disciples?' Peter was startled and confused; the eyes of the company instantly fastened upon him. He pretended not to understand her; but she was persistent, and said to those around her that this man was with Jesus. Peter felt compelled to answer, and said angrily, 'Woman, I know Him not.' This was the first denial" *(The Desire of Ages*, pp. 710, 711). Twice more Peter denied his Lord. The last time he began to swear. I don't think he had sworn for years. But he was flustered and afraid for himself. He panicked.

Then the cock crowed, and his soul awoke to the horror of what he had done. To crown his agony, he looked up to see his Savior watching him. "That look of Christ's broke his heart. Peter had come to the turning point, and bitterly did he repent his sin. . . . The look of Christ assured him of pardon. Now his self-confidence was gone. Never again were the old boastful assertions repeated. . . . The once restless, boastful, self-confident disciple had become subdued and contrite. Henceforth he followed his Lord in self-denial and self-sacrifice. . . . Peter's fall was not instantaneous, but gradual. Self-confidence led him to the belief that he was saved, and step after step was taken in the downward path, until he could deny his Master. . . . It was through self-sufficiency that Peter fell; and it was through repentance and humiliation that his feet were again established" (*Christ's Object Lessons,* pp. 154, 155).

That Sabbath during which Christ rested in the tomb must have been the bitterest in Simon's life. Leaving the judgment hall, Peter returned to Gethsemane. Prostrate with remorse, he poured out his soul in repentance and lifted up his heart in prayer. Like Christ he wet the sod with his tears. Perhaps he went back to Calvary and looked at the cross. Lest Peter should feel that he was no longer appreciated by his Lord, on Sunday morning the Savior sent a special message to him. When announcing through the women who visited the sepulcher His appointment with His followers, the angel bade them, "Go . . ., tell his disciples and Peter" (Mark 16:7). Some time later Jesus sought Simon out alone and had a special visit with him (Luke 24:34; 1 Cor. 15:5) to comfort him and to assure him of forgiveness and acceptance.

While Peter had turned his back on fishing he evidently still had access to a ship. Perhaps it was lying in some shallow cove on Galilee's lake. "I go fishing," he remarked to the disciples, and off they all had gone. He still can lead! The boat is bailed out, the sail is put up, and out they go to fish. But they catch nothing. This was to remind Peter of his call. At that time too he had caught no fish, but "at thy word" (Luke 5:5), as he put it, he had tried again. Then he had been made a fisher of men. Now Jesus met them once more and told them to fish again. They did so and caught a great school. This time Jesus made Peter a shepherd.

When this crisis was all over, Christ tested Peter's devotion. In words by the lakeside, so reminiscent of his original call, the Master asked, "Lovest thou me?" Three times, with pointed emphasis, Peter acknowledged his Lord (John 21:15-19). This was to neutralize the three times he had denied Him.

In the upper room Peter is still leader (Acts 1:15). By common consent he is reinstated. Try to get into Peter's heart as he stands up to record officially the betrayal and death of Judas, and to propose the election of his successor (verses 16-22). Peter had also betrayed his Lord. Yet he is there preaching while the other is in Aceldama. In the courage it must have taken to make this speech let us measure the man. He knew what it meant to betray and to find his way back through mercy. Peter understood the power of Christ's grace. He was thus fitted to say what the Spirit used him to say.

And on Pentecost we see Peter again. He stands boldly and fearlessly. We watch amazed as he indicts his whole Hebrew nation for the crime they have committed. They have betrayed the Son of God. So had he. It was this understanding that helped him to turn them into the road of safety and salvation. Peter spoke from experience and conviction and firsthand knowledge. Only thus could his words have proved effective. And how effective they were! Three thousand were swept from denial and betrayal and murder of God's Son to repentance and humility and acceptance of Christ as their Savior.

We note Peter, with his companion John, continuing to work for their people. The early chapters of the book of Acts are familiar to us. He who had denied his Lord rejoiced to suffer persecution. Back in the court of the high priest, Peter was ready to witness for his Lord with a boldness second to none. This finds a parallel only in the vehemence with which he had betrayed Him. "The cause of Christ would often have suffered had it been left to John alone. Peter's zeal was needed. His boldness and energy often delivered them from difficulty and silenced their enemies" (*Early Writings,* p. 225).

Peter was also a theologian. All through his experience with the living Christ he had longed to understand. It was he who first declared his faith in the divinity of Jesus at Caesarea Philippi (Matt. 16:13-19). He also wanted to be told about future rewards (Mark 10:28). And he was troubled as to the number of times forgiveness should be extended to an erring brother (Matt. 18:21, 22). He was curious and remarked upon the strange case of the withered fig tree (Mark 11:21). He often asked Jesus questions. The answers he obtained helped the disciples, and us, to understand. They clarify our grasp of the things of the kingdom of God. We owe his curiosity a great debt of gratitude. Peter had come a long way when he wrote his Epistles. He was ready to concede humbly that some things in the writings of Paul were too profound for him to understand. How different is this from those who claim to be his successors!

In the spreading shadows about the cross we may see Peter's tear-stained and haggard face. His repentance and remorse led him eagerly to seek to be right with his Master once more. He strove to make up for the great wrong he had done Him by devoting his life to uncomplaining dedication and service. In him we may see a dim reflection of ourselves. We deny. We betray. We sometimes try to prove that the strait and narrow ways of the Nazarene are things to be joked about! But his life's experiences bring us hope. They set in marked contrast the mercy and patience and forgiving compassion of the Savior we revere. Let us yield to Him now and save ourselves the remorse of tomorrow.

Chapter 7

Judas the Covetous

Smart Follower—"How Much?"

And then there was a traitor whose sinister shadow added to the darkness surrounding the cross. He is universally execrated. His name has become a byword for baseless treachery. His notoriety rests on his betrayal of his avowed Lord. Today the very name Judas drips with hypocrisy, sneaking, self-seeking, violence, and black murder. If Judas had any good qualities—and he must have had or Christ would never have included him among the twelve—they have long since sunk beneath the slime of his final actions.

Judas held the highest social position among the apostles. He was a "scribe," and is introduced to us namelessly. "While Jesus was preparing the disciples for their ordination, one who had not been summoned urged his presence among them. It was Judas Iscariot, a man who professed to be a follower of Christ. He now came forward, soliciting a place in this inner circle of disciples. With great earnestness and apparent sincerity he declared, 'Master, I will follow thee whithersoever thou goest.' Jesus neither repulsed nor welcomed him, but uttered only the mournful words: 'The foxes have holes, and the birds of the air have nests; but the Son of man hath not where to lay His head' (Matt. 8:19, 20). Judas believed Jesus to be the Messiah; and by joining the apostles, he hoped to secure a high position in the new kingdom" (*The Desire of Ages,* pp. 292, 293).

Jesus understood Judas' disposition and need perfectly. His

reply to Judas' suggestion was, in effect, "Stop, and think carefully. If you do, you will grow by the effort. And let Me warn you: There will be no wealth or comfort coming your way if you identify yourself with Me."

Our Lord's words to aspiring Judas appear almost curt. Yet here, at the very outset, Jesus plainly warned him that there was nothing of worldly gain or personal comfort to be gained from becoming a disciple of such a Master.

The words with which Judas approached Jesus are revealing. They seem to betoken an intense, highly strung, almost impetuous character. They tell of a slave to impulse and feeling. Christ showed by His reply that He understood this perfectly well. Yet Judas had sensed in Jesus something which drew him to his Lord. The better qualities of his nature felt the force of our Savior's dynamic attractiveness.

Judas was also deeply conscious of the truth and wonder of Jesus' words. "He felt the influence of that divine power which was drawing souls to the Savior" (*ibid.*, p. 294). Deep and wide must have been this appeal. For even those Temple guards sent to arrest Jesus affirmed in awe, "Never man spake like this man" (John 7:46).

Let us consider the sort of person Judas was. He possessed a mind of his own. He was prepared to break away from his old associations and friends. This trait was as evident in the later betrayal of his Master as in his initial avowal of His cause. Sanctified, this quality would have been a great asset in strengthening Judas to set aside public opinion in favor of taking his stand on the side of truth. It would also have encouraged the more wavering among the disciples to a steadfast and holy boldness.

Coupled with this independence of mind, Judas possessed what might have become another virtue. He fearlessly expressed his opinions, regardless of whether they courted pleasure or censure (John 12:4-8). He was also able to organize public opinion favorable to himself and the enterprise he advocated. All these traits are valuable to a large degree in truly converted disciples. They would have proved effective if used rightly in the cause of Him whom Judas had termed Lord. Unconsecrated, they led their possessor to the vilest treachery, which has garbed his memory with a loathing that has grown through the passing centuries into utter revulsion.

The Lord saw clearly all that Judas might have accomplished, as well as what he actually did (John 6:64). "The Savior read the heart of Judas; He knew the depths of iniquity to which, unless delivered by the grace of God, Judas would sink" (*ibid*). By extending His call to him, He gave confidence to an erratic follower. By His encouragement and help through the years of their association, Jesus did His best to exorcise the "devil" Judas cherished in his heart. What more risky, more lovingly generous gesture could Jesus have made to humanity than this? Could any act have more movingly demonstrated His confidence in the possibility of improvement in the human heart? What could have better stimulated the sidetracked to the sublimation of their instinctive tendencies to highest idealism?

That Judas, and with him many of us, should eventually betray this confidence discredits our Lord not one whit. Rather, since we acknowledge that Jesus knew well the end of Judas' course, it enhances His characteristic of patient and tolerant love.

Judas was surnamed Iscariot, that is, "man of Kerioth," a town in southern Palestine. He would thus be a Judean. Possibly because of his wealth or social position, Judas was entrusted with the care of the slender resources shared by the disciples (John 13:29).

In the episodes in which Judas' name appears in the Gospel

story we are given the steps of his declension. He criticized and complained at Mary's generous gesture in the house of Simon the leper. The motive that prompted his hypocritical outburst is clearly set down. Judas cried indignantly, "Why was not this ointment sold for three hundred pence, and given to the poor?" John explains the significance of this in an aside: "This he said, not that he cared for the poor; but because he was a thief, and had the bag, and bare [stole] what was put therein" (John 12:5, 6; cf. Matt. 26:8; Mark 14:4). Knowing the poverty of the disciples, aware of Mary's joy in forgiveness, and conscious of Jesus as his Lord, Judas could, notwithstanding, boldly advocate a policy that would ultimately benefit none but himself. "He was a thief." What a cold, calculating thief he was, too!

Jesus did not openly rebuke the traitor, although He knew perfectly well the thoughts that were in his heart. "How tenderly the Savior dealt with him who was to be His betrayer! In His teaching, Jesus dwelt upon principles of benevolence that struck at the very root of covetousness. He presented before Judas the heinous character of greed, and many a time the disciple realized that his character had been portrayed, and his sin pointed out; but he would not confess and forsake his unrighteousness. He was self-sufficient, and instead of resisting temptation, he continued to follow his fraudulent practices. Christ was before him, a living example of what he must become if he reaped the benefit of the divine mediation and ministry. . . . Instead of walking in the light, Judas chose to retain his defects. Evil desires, revengeful passions, dark and sullen thoughts, were cherished, until Satan had full control of the man. Judas became a representative of the enemy of Christ.

"When he came into association with Jesus, he had some precious traits of character that might have been made a blessing to the church. If he had been willing to wear the yoke of Christ, he might have been among the chief of the apostles; but he hardened his heart when his defects were pointed out, and in pride and rebellion chose his own selfish ambitions, and thus unfitted himself for the work that God would have given him to *do" (ibid.*, p. 295).

Self-seeking and its twin, jealousy, mastered Judas. He finally reached the conclusion that there was nothing to be gained from continuing his association with Jesus and the disciples. True to the character his selfishness had matured, he determined to get as much out of the break as he could.

His social connections with the members of the Sanhedrin enabled Judas to hear of their plotting against the Savior. The resurrection of Lazarus finally crystallized the purpose of Israel's hierarchy to destroy Jesus by any means opportunity might present and their cumulative ingenuity suggest.

At this point Judas decided to sell his Lord to these plotters. Concealing his true purpose, he came and went as before. Unknown to the disciples, he brought his dark schemes to a ripe state of preparedness. Carefully he bargained with the chief priests, exacting his price, 30 pieces of silver (Matt. 26:15). Ironical and moving is this figure, the price of a slave (Ex. 21:32)! He who came to free all bondmen, to break every fetter, to loose every band, was sold for the price of one of these! And He was done to death in the moment of His transacting their final liberation!

And even after He knew Judas had laid his plan, Jesus gave the betrayer opportunity after opportunity to change his purpose. He washed the feet of Judas as a token of the cleansing that he was refusing. He warned Judas that He fully knew what he contemplated doing (John 13:21-30). And when the darkness of eternal night finally settled upon the heart of the ill-starred man of Kerioth it was not without ample and patient admonition and warning.

All the details of the final betrayal sicken and revolt. The act that plumbs the very depths of human depravity is the sign by which Judas proposed to identify Jesus. He kissed Him (Matt. 26:49). The whole gamut of human history presents no more filthy kiss and unholy embrace than that of Judas the prostitute. And our blessed Lord suffered that hot, hairy, fanatical face to kiss His! Yet, even at the last moment, Jesus tried to spare Judas this final gesture that should damn him throughout all ages. Christ revealed Himself through the request "Whom seek ye?" (John 18:4).

The heavenly calm of Christ in the face of this revolting contact is magnificent. Undisturbed, He said, "Friend, why are you here?'" (Matt. 26:50, RSV). And then inquired as if to shock Judas out of his plan even at this eleventh hour, "Betrayest thou the Son of man with a kiss?" (Luke 22:48).

Something of that final contact with his Lord broke Judas. His condition was not that of Peter when he realized what he had done. The pride of Judas led him to a remorse-filled suicide and ignoble end. As one has observed:

"Mine own apostle, who the bag did beare,

Though he had all I had, did not forbeare,

To sell Me also, and to put Me there."

He who might have done great things for God passed to an unmarked grave, his memory despised wherever his story is told.

Among those who watched Christ die stands this greedy, thieving, selfish, avaricious man, who was even ready to sell his Savior for a paltry sum. Sometimes we wonder why he did not demand more. But today we betray for trifles the principles for which Christ stands. Compromise with sin, association with worthless companions, dishonesty in the hours we work for the wages we earn—all these may seem trifles. But are they our price of betrayal?

Are we among the faceless ones about the cross who suddenly take on identity when we look in the mirror? The shadow of Judas the treacherous flits in the dark areas about the Crucified. Do we ever identify with him?

Chapter 8

Centurion the Conscientious

Heathen Executioner—"Truly This Was the Son of God"

The man charged with the execution was the captain of the Roman guard. His command numbered perhaps 65 men. Tradition suggests that his name was Longinus.

What he had done before he arrived in Palestine we do not know. He might have volunteered for this tour of duty. Those soldiers of fortune who came to such a troubled spot knew what to expect. Danger lurked behind the boulders of the desert. Patriotism was equated with killing a Roman. Others covered their crimes against the government with the cloak of political zeal. They were bigots at heart who would have been bigots at any time. But in these days of nationalism a Jew could always count on sympathy through anti-Roman activities.

A centurion was ever on the alert for unexpected ambushes. He handled the local citizens roughly. That was part of his duty. He lived in a violent age in a violent land and dealt with violent people. Pilate, the Roman governor, was a cruel man. His sentiments distilled through the ranks of those who enforced his decisions.

This Paschal Friday morning Longinus was ordered to see that three men died by means of the regular grisly ceremony. I don't think that this was the first time he had carried out the ritual of death. He and his men probably knew just what to do. The crosses were prepared. A squad of men was assigned to each prisoner. Longinus superintended the guards who kept the crowds in order. There were many different kinds of people milling around the slowly moving throng. Weeping women stood side by side with jeering priests and sadistic men. Many are always attracted to an execution. Some come because of morbid, cowardly interest in the dying. Perhaps they feel their own guilt being punished in the condemned. Others were curious. Some happened by and joined the crowds.

The procession moved awkwardly through the narrow streets of Jerusalem. It passed out of a city gate and on to Old Skull Face. I don't think that Longinus needed to speak much on the way. His men were well drilled. They were carefully disciplined. They had their orders. He kept abreast of the prisoners. Always alert, he watched for any unfriendly movement, especially lest some friend of the criminals attempt a last-minute rescue. But nothing like this happened.

At Golgotha the fight with the thieves was soon over. Powerful hands soon had them pinioned, tied, and nailed. Longinus must have been amazed as he noted that Jesus made no resistance. He lay down without a struggle. He submitted to the nails without flinching. And as His cross was lifted and plunged with great violence into the hole prepared for it, no curse, but only a prayer, escaped His lips. The centurion superintended the placing of a legend over each of the criminals. This contained his name and the crimes for which he was paying the supreme penalty. This was the last act in the weird and cruel drama.

Longinus relaxed for the first time that morning. Matthew tells us that he and his soldiers prepared for their long vigil as the men on the crosses slowly died. I doubt whether the two thieves attracted the attention of Longinus. He had seen too many of their kind. Jesus was the focus of his interest. He had no fear that He might even now escape. But something about the fortitude of this Nazarene attracted the Roman centurion. The look of pain on His face had given place to one of serene trust. Every time He moved His head the rough cross would press the spikes of the crown of thorns into His flesh. But He spoke no word of complaint. The nails were tearing ever-widening holes in His gaping hands and feet. I don't think Jesus moved much. But He prayed, "Father, forgive them; for they know not what they do." Longinus knew, or thought he knew, exactly what he was doing! He must have been satisfied that he had carried out his orders well. There was no possibility of his ghastly work being undone! "Father, forgive . . ." The voice he had heard, the majesty in the lacerated body on the cross, arrested and gripped his attention further. Something was pulling him out of himself.

Longinus had probably not heard Jesus make His grand declaration of authority: "I, if I be lifted up from the earth, will draw all men unto me" (John 12:32). But he was certainly feeling its power. In spite of himself he was being mightily attracted to the Figure on the central cross. The hours slowly crawled by. Those at the foot of the gibbet passed the time by gambling for bloody garments. Did Longinus see that seamless robe? Did he think of the loving mother whose hands had woven it for her Son? One of the soldiers decided not to tear it up; it looked too good. He argued that it would fetch a better price at the pawnshop if left intact. "Who'll roll some dice for it?" he called. And so they had cast lots, and the robe of God's great high priest stayed seamless and intact. Did Caiaphas, high priest in the Temple at Jerusalem, wonder? Did he remember the ancient law that forbade a high priest's robe from being rent on any account? Did he sense, even vaguely, that he had rent his office and forfeited his responsibility and broken God's law by his rash act in rending his robe? His authority had thus been ended. Did he sense dimly that Christ, God's high priest, now had supreme authority? But Caiaphas might have sought to justify himself. His voice might have joined in the jeering taunt, "He saved others: himself he cannot save" (Matt. 27:42).

Did Longinus have any knowledge of Christ? He had read the name Jesus on the placard. Did he know it meant Savior? Had he heard Christ's claims to be the Son of God? Longinus must have looked at Him with new interest.

The centurion had probably stood by Pilate and heard the governor say in amazement, "Behold the Man!" Never had such a One stood before the Roman judge—One mighty in His weakness, omnipotent in His crucifixion, His cross a throne, His thorns the crown of the universe. As Longinus stood there watching, God drew the blinds. The sun went out, and it was dark. No eye must see the closing moments of Christ's death. Longinus was no longer concerned with the figures leaning forward in agony from the crosses. But he was on the alert lest some disciple seek to snatch Jesus away. Perhaps he ordered his soldiers to be more vigilant.

Longinus probably heard the words of Jesus to the thief. Then came the request, "I thirst." Some soldier took a cane. He fixed a sponge to its end. Dipped in sour wine, it was pressed to the parched lips of Jesus. But the priests mocked his agony. "Let be," they said, "let us see whether Elias will come to save him" (Matt. 27:49; cf. *The Desire of Ages,* pp. 754, 755).

And then the centurion heard the triumphant cry "It is finished," and the words of self-committal: "Father, into thy hands I commend my spirit" (Luke 23:46). What did these words mean? There was a great earthquake. And when the centurion heard the voice and saw the earthquake and the things that were done, he said, "Certainly this was a righteous man" (Luke 23:47). "Truly this was the Son of God" (Matt. 27:54).

"This was a righteous" Man, "This was the Son of God." Can anyone, anywhere, theologian or simple believer, say more about Jesus?

Longinus now knew that Jesus was the most righteous man he had ever known. He also knew He was God's Son, divine. In this witness the Roman centurion acknowledged that Jesus of Nazareth was God-man, the Incarnate. "The divine patience of the Savior, and His sudden death, with the cry of victory upon His lips, had impressed this heathen. In the bruised, broken body hanging upon the cross, the centurion recognized the form of the Son of God. He could not refrain from confessing his faith. Thus again evidence was given that our Redeemer was to see of the travail of His soul. Upon the very day of His death, three men, differing widely from one another, had declared their faith—he who commanded the Roman guard, he who bore the cross of the Savior, and he who died upon the cross at His side" (*The Desire of Ages,* p. 770). Christ's prayer, Christ's drawing power, were each triumphant.

The least likely of men, the superintendent of executioners, the professional killer of criminals, believed! There at the foot of the cross heaven was opened to him. He accepted the Son of God as his ladder leading him to the higher life.

We may ascend this ladder too. Does the thought cross your mind, I can't come to Jesus; I can't pray? I'm not good enough? I can't stretch up and touch Him whom I long to reach, that I might be cleansed and freed and healed? Jesus is tugging at your heart right now. Acknowledge Him, the Man among men. Jesus is praying for you, "Father, forgive them; they know not what they do." Call Him your God. Accept Him as king in your life. Take Him as your example. Praise Him for His dying, His living, His pleading. Testify that you believe. He will take the unblemished robe of His matchless character and cast it about your poor nakedness and filth. All its loveliness may be yours now. He is touched with every twinge of your pain. He sympathizes with every feeling in your lonely heart. He will come into your mind and give you His peace and power. Take Him at His word.

You may not feel intensely about it yet. That doesn't matter. We don't operate by feeling. We humans have will and choice. It really doesn't matter what we feel about this. You can, right now, will to make yourself a child of God. Jesus awaits your choice. Move from reason to decision. Operate by the sovereign of your life, your mind. Will to surrender to the Spirit, and He will make you more than conqueror.

Jesus took that cruel, callous, unfeeling Roman officer and changed him into another man. Longinus the conscientious had done what he considered his duty. Jesus drew his efforts into the highest channels. The Roman soldier observed the evidences that Jesus was God-man. He yielded to these evidences. His heart's cry might have been "God, make me like Him." Calvary achieved this for him. What is it doing for you? Put your will on the side of Jesus. Give Him your life. When feelings come up, say, "Not mine, but Thy will be done." Yield to the tug of the Crucified. Jesus is on His throne. His is the crown of universal sovereignty. It is made of thorns that are my curse. The scepter of supreme authority is in His hand. It is the reed that I used to strike Him. But He still loves me. His love is everlasting. It takes in each of us. Put yourself on His side now. Keep yourself on His side forever. Peace in time and joy in eternity are yours, "more than you can ask or think." The centurion the conscientious joins his voice to invite you, through the cross, to the Christ. "He being dead, yet speaketh."

Chapter 9

John the Confused

Foster Brother—"Our Hands Have Handled"

John preeminently wrote of Christ as the Son of God. His descriptions of Jesus as the preexistent One are among the most moving and profound statements found in all literature.

The designation this evangelist applies to himself in his writing is the disciple "whom Jesus loved" (John 13:23), and he certainly reciprocated the affection the Savior lavished upon him. "We love him," he wrote at the end of his long life, "because he first loved us" (1 John 4:19).

We often think of John as possessed of the affectionate, saintly character in which he emerges from his Epistles. We forget that he was not always thus. Naturally he had grave defects. "He was proud and ambitious, and quick to resent slight and injury" (*The Sanctified Life*, p. 41). John was most deeply conscious that his Savior had loved him in spite of these weaknesses. And because of this fact he was strongly attracted to the Son of man.

John apparently had been a follower of the Baptist (John 1:35-40). The main points of this harbinger's preaching were repentance of sin and preparation for the coming Messiah. All who adhered to John the Baptist would therefore feel the urge for an amendment of life springing from a deep consciousness of personal sin. John Boanerges (Mark 3:17) longed for this reformation. In his yearning for emancipation from guilt he was prepared to go wherever the quest might lead him.

When the Baptist finally identified the Savior, John was ready to leave his first master. Although he had felt a rich affection for the Baptist, John was prepared to throw in his lot with the disciples of the Messiah. But there were many of the followers of the Baptist who refused to follow Christ. There are always those whose current spiritual experiences give them so much satisfaction that they refuse to advance into greater light and fuller truth. Of such our Lord declared, "No man also having drunk old wine straightway desireth new: for he saith, The old is better" (Luke 5:39). John was clear thinking enough and strong willed enough to go forward, however joyful had been past experiences with the Baptist.

When John finally left his life's occupation to follow Jesus, the Gospel narrative informs us that he forsook his father and his hired servants. These facts give us a glimpse into his family's economic status. They point to the wrench in filial affection that the call of Christ must have entailed. He who had seen in Jesus the vision of his need, and for this considered all creature comforts subordinate, naturally would love his Lord with all his heart.

John was ever ready to elbow his way into the very forefront of the band. He was prepared to parade his qualities, and was eager, by open demonstration, to vindicate his pretentions to preeminence.

John was zealous for the cause of the Messiah, to whom he had given loyalty. On one occasion he reported to Jesus his reaction to a stranger whom he had seen "casting out devils" in Jesus' name. He had immediately forbidden him to do so (Mark 9:38-40). John evidently had felt that an outsider might bring disrepute upon the cause of Christ. Here was one who apparently had not forsaken all to follow Jesus, who, nevertheless, gathered to himself the approbation of the multitudes. We see in John the workings of a fiery bigot.

Later in the ministry of the Messiah, John manifested a similar weakness. While on His final way to Jerusalem, Jesus passed through Samaria. Perceiving that the miracle-working Christ was bent on passing Gerizim in favor of Moriah, the Samaritans refused to receive the Lord and His disciples. Incensed at this, John requested permission to call down fire upon the Samaritans as Elijah had done on his enemies (Luke 9:51-56). The same motives, jealousy and zeal, still combined to stir the heart of John. Gently Jesus tried to turn the fiery disciple's mind into a more charitable and forgiving relationship with his fellow human beings.

Jesus' dealings with John were wonderfully patient. He granted special privileges to His young disciple. In Jesus, John watched God in action. He learned, firsthand, that Christ could grant life (Luke 8:46-56). He saw his Lord in glory with Moses and Elijah, who had come from the skies. He listened to them discussing with the Savior the death He was to consummate in Jerusalem (Matt. 17:1, 2). He witnessed the crisis that was the culmination of our Lord's victory, when in Gethsemane the fate of humanity was decided (Mark 14:32, 33). John plumbed the depths of God's plan for humanity's redemption, and was thus able to rise to the very highest revealed knowledge of the Deity. Like a tree that grows taller as its roots strike deeper, John grew and flourished.

John was the only disciple who lingered about the cross. The Lord chose him as the foster son and supporter of His mother, through whose heart the sword was in the very act of passing (John 19:27). In the further development of his character Mary may have exercised a not-inconsiderable influence.

This woman had held God's Son close to her heart. She had cherished what prophet and angel had disclosed concerning His destiny. She would surely share her understanding with John, who himself, while leaning on the breast of the Son of man, had listened to the deep beating of that mighty heart of love. Mary, who had been entrusted by the Father with the training of His Son, could not but profoundly mold and fashion the mind and character of a man as affectionate and impressionable as was the youngest of the apostles, John.

And on the morning of the resurrection John was the first of the disciples to reach the open tomb. His love shone through the gloom of that awful weekend.

After Pentecost we again see John in Samaria (Acts 8:14-17). He is calling down fire upon the villagers, but now the fire is that of God's Holy Spirit. One may discern in this a parable of the entire change in John's life. His energies, previously used to destroy and decry, have now been directed to the highest and finest enterprises. He longed to sit on the throne of Christ. In spirit he has been enabled to reveal to humanity the inestimable privileges of sonship. In the unveiling of Jesus on His Father's throne the apostle has carried men from merely terrestrial things to the very presence of the Eternal. Through his heart, by means of his pen, Jesus is displayed in all His loveliness.

In John's young face, so pained by the tortures of his dying Lord, we see love and fear mingled. He was dreadfully sorry for his flight in the night of arrest. So he continued to linger about the cross on Calvary. Feeling so helpless, he longed to be able to do something for his Master. Then it was that the Savior entrusted His mother to him.

We would love to have such a task. And so to us the word

of Jesus whispers across the centuries, "Inasmuch as ye have done it unto one of the least of these my brethren, ye have done it unto me" (Matt. 25:40). Can you see a needy soul by the cross, borne down with grief, in dire need? The word is "Inasmuch." As you serve him, you serve his Lord and yours. In John selfishness gave way to service at the cross. May the example of his life be ours.

Chapter 10

Thief the Converted

Lad Who Strayed—"Remember Me"

Let us look at this drama of Calvary through another man's eyes. I imagine something like this might have happened. He had heard Jesus preach. We don't know his name; we only know what he did. As the Savior ministered to the sick and the needy, he might have been standing on the outskirts of the crowd. Perhaps, like other young people, with heaven a long way away and righteousness a theory, he had laughed and joked with his friends, but he had listened a little bit. His exuberance made a way for him with other boon companions. Life was all fun! Each day held its chance to have a good time. He and his buddies became more and more daring. The simple routine no longer held anything exciting. The law stood as a challenge. He and his companions vied with one another to flout its restrictions.

Then, one day, the long arm of a Roman soldier was laid across his path. He had been arrested and condemned to death. Now things looked altogether different, tougher, harder. The initial thought that he was to die hit him like a hammer! His sentence had been pronounced, and now he was on death row, waiting. Some morning he would be led out and killed. It was happening to him! He had heard that it had happened to others, but now it was his turn to be executed.

And then the morning arrived. Let us imagine that instead of being taken directly to the place of death, he and his two fellow criminals were led back to the judgment hall of the Roman governor. This time there was something different in the proceedings. There was another Prisoner standing in the dock. The judge was talking of an exchange of criminals. Gradually the thief realized that the ringleader of a band of malefactors was to be released! How well he knew what a hard, cruel, murderous renegade Barabbas was! He gathered that Barabbas was to be released in the place of the other Prisoner! And when his eyes focused on this other, there was nothing but incredulity and amazement in his heart.

Could it be that the Preacher and Barabbas were to change places? The Miracle Worker was to die and the murderer was to go free? The Gentle Blesser of children was to be nailed to the tree and a rebel and curse to men was to be set free? But the road to Golgotha was too short for the thoughts that might have crowded one another in his mind. He knew from experience the effect of the scourging; he knew what the second scourging meant to the Man of Nazareth. There must have been sympathy in his heart as he watched Simon, the farmer, carry the cross of Jesus. And by that time they were there.

The distance from Pilate's judgment hall to Calvary is not far. Whichever location you select for it, traditional or the one more probable, the distance is short to the Place of a Skull. And now they were binding him to put him to death. He and his fellow prisoner wrestled with their executioners. It is a very unpleasant picture. The fight soon ended. A heavy knee was slammed on his chest. Strong arms held him down. He was tied and nailed. With his cross he was lifted unsteadily up. He lurched forward as the cross dropped into the hole prepared for it. The pain almost made him drift into unconsciousness. But his mind swam back into focus. Yes, he was being slowly killed.

What were his thoughts that moment when, at his feet, the

unresisting Nazarene was also being crucified? The thief had cursed. He had called down imprecations on the heads of the judge, his companions, his executioners. But then the confusion was halted for a moment. A quiet voice prayed, "Father, forgive them; for they know not what they do." Then his understanding came alive like a surging flood. The memories of all he had heard this Preacher say rose before him in waves of comprehension. Life's way suddenly took a completely different turn. In his memory he was back home, and his mother was telling him the old stories that mothers in Israel had told their boys for hundreds of years. I like to imagine that these were stories of bad men becoming good; of good men becoming perfect; and of some good men becoming bad. The mothers in Israel tried to give reasons for all this, but I imagine the warnings to their boys and girls sometimes fell on hearts that disbelieved or were indifferent.

"King Saul was a big man, bigger than any man in Israel," I can hear her say. "And the Holy Spirit came into his heart and made him into a new person. He who could freely roam the mountains unafraid was changed into a prophet divinely disciplined. And his friends began joking with one another, 'Saul is a prophet! Saul is a prophet!' He was the last man, they had imagined, who would ever become a preacher! And then Saul became king. But he didn't pray; he didn't read the Scriptures; he didn't learn to trust God and obey His will each day. Yet God continued to bless him. But in spite of this he became proud. He felt he could do everything by himself. He didn't need God. He didn't need God's priest. He didn't need God's prophet or His preacher. And so a man whom God had made good made himself bad by leaving God out of his life." Some such way her little story must have been told.

"Then there was Samson, a baby announced by the angel to

his mother before ever he was born, who grew into manhood and became so strong that no one was as strong as he. But Samson made the wrong friends. He didn't play with the boys and girls whose mothers and fathers wanted them to do right—not Samson! They were too goody-goody for him. He made friends with boys and girls whose fathers and mothers didn't care about God; who didn't even worship God; who never prayed in their homes; who never went to church. And soon Samson began to do the same things these boys and girls did. Samson's mother was grief-stricken. Samson must have come home several times and seen his mother crying. Perhaps he even heard his mother tell him, 'Samson, you are going to break my heart one of these days. Why do you do that? Don't you love your mother enough to stop your wicked ways?'" And so the dying thief's mother might have talked to her boy.

On the cross the young criminal remembered it all. He had done just that. He had broken his mother's heart. He knew he had. His dad had looked 10 years older when he first came to visit him in jail. He now thought of the elder in the synagogue who had put his hand on his head when he was a little boy and had said, "Son, when you grow up, be like your dad, serve your God." But he hadn't. He had made friends with those who were not friends of God. And now he was being killed and the blood was dripping from the nail wounds, and he was remembering everything, but there was nothing he could do about it. He couldn't pull his hands away from those spikes. He couldn't pull his legs away from those iron barbs. He couldn't move, because it hurt too much, and soon he was going to die.

Around him was utter confusion. Multitudes were there jabbering and laughing and swearing. His companion, a few feet away, was cursing, just as he knew how. But what good was it now? I wonder whether he thought of that board meeting that might well have been held in the synagogue, at which the elder may have said something like this: "It is a very painful duty that falls on me. We all know the sad history of one of our young members. Murder has been done with robbery. I am afraid we must take his name off the synagogue book." Tears had been shed, and he knew that he was the cause of those tears.

I wonder whether his mother and father were standing in the crowd praying for their boy. There was another mother there, and she was praying, as she had prayed all her life, for her Boy. But now His hour had come, and He was on the cross too. And the sword was even going through her heart. And then, perhaps, the thief could stand it no longer. He called out to his companion, "Stop! Why are you cursing and swearing? We are getting what we deserve. This Man has done nothing amiss." He knew what was right. And he knew what was wrong. And he knew the Preacher by his side was right.

And now Luke takes up the story of the thief. "And he said unto Jesus, Lord, remember me when thou comest into thy kingdom" (Luke 23:42). Everything had come together in a wonderful solution to life's problems. A light was shining in the thief's mind. All the stories he had heard, all the sermons he had listened to, all the messages that he had read in the Scriptures—they now fitted together with wonderful meaning. "This is He whom the prophets have predicted," he might have said to himself. "This Man is certainly the Messiah whose kingdom is about to be established." He knew it!

Jesus made reply in words that are forever movingly memorable. "Truly, I say to you today," when I am nearly dead, He might have added, when it appears as if My kingdom has been crumbled into ruin by the hammer blows of those who crucify, when I have come to My own nation and they have rejected Me, when I have chosen 12 apostles and one has betrayed, one has denied, and 10 have fled from Me, today, I affirm on my divine authority, when it looks like the end, but is actually the beginning, because of your faith in Me, "you shall be with Me in Paradise."

Jesus did not go to Paradise that day. In a few hours His body was taken down from the cross and gently laid in garments of purest white. His body was anointed with spikenard. His lacerated hands and feet, scarred head, bleeding side, and loving heart were still. He was placed in Joseph's new tomb. And all the next day, the Sabbath, He rested. Very early in the morning of the first day of the week, called to life by His Father's authority, resuming eternal life by His own power, He was to return to His Father's home in Paradise. But He delayed. He could see coming up the Bethany Road a shrouded figure. As the trees took form in the brightening dawn, as the darkness disappeared on the wings of light, and as the sun of a new day spilled its thin brilliance across the landscape, He waited.

Into the Garden, distressed beyond words, the figure stumbled. Blinded by tears, distracted by sorrow, Mary returned to the tomb she had visited earlier. It was empty! Disconsolate and sobbing, she stumbled back. Nearby she saw a figure. Thinking Him to be the gardener, she blurted out, "Sir, if thou have borne him hence, tell me where thou hast laid him, and I will take him away" (John 20:15). Have you ever wondered where she would have placed Christ's body? What could she have done with it? In this story we should look at her love for Jesus. She loved Him with an abandon that in her grief was almost irrational. And then the Figure said one gentle word: "Mary!" Immediately she fell in adoration at His feet, which she had once kissed and bathed with her tears and dried with her tresses. He had accepted her homage before. But now He would receive none of her worship, though He deserved it even more. "Touch me not," he warned kindly; "for I am not yet ascended to my Father."

Christ had not yet gone to Paradise at that point on the Sunday morning. So the day on which He had promised eternal life to the dying thief could not be the day He had intended him to go to Paradise. That day had been the day of His humiliation. But it was also the day of His authority. His hour had come, and in His death He would triumph. His seeming impotence on the cross would give place to power illimitable. He who had been scourged and dragged and bound and nailed would carry the government of God on His shoulder forever. And His kingdom would have no end.

But let's go back to that Friday afternoon when the thief was on the cross. The central figure of the three was silent in death. The other two still lived. "The Jews therefore, because it was the preparation, that the bodies should not remain upon the cross on the Sabbath day, (for the sabbath day was a high day,) besought Pilate that their legs might be broken, and that they might be taken away. Then came the soldiers, and brake the legs of the first, and of the other which was crucified with him" (John 19:31, 32). He whom we call the thief on the cross must have waited in horror for his turn. How they broke his legs we are not told. But when they had been smashed he was jerked from the cross. He still lived, for he was young and strong. Someone may have tied a rope around his ankle, and fastened the other end to a donkey, and so dragged him to Jerusalem's rubbish heap. And through it all he still lived. He might well have lingered between life and death for days. Then blood poisoning, fever, weakness, finally destroyed him.

What do you think he thought of Christ's promise, "I say

unto thee to day, shalt thou be with me in paradise?" How did he feel that Sabbath evening when the sun went down in darkness, only to rise again and to smite him with its heat during the ensuing day? There was no one there to respond to his cry "I thirst!" even with a sponge of sour wine. But he must have held on to Christ's promise by faith, for the promise to have been fulfilled at all.

Sometimes we think the thief on the cross had an easy time, that he simply died and was at once at peace, awaiting the resurrection morn. Let us open our eyes and our spirits to sympathize and understand. How long he lay tossing in pain until he died, I know not. But even if it was two days, three days, in the horrors of those closing hours he endured all the anguish of a normal lifetime. During those final moments he exercised all the sustaining faith of an ordinary life.

I wonder whether his father or mother had heard Christ's promise. I doubt it. The executioners who signed the record in the guardroom, certifying that he had been duly executed, gave little or no thought to it. In their register he was just another entry, another accessory of robbers who had paid the price. But in heaven's book there was a place of honor for him. One day that dust will be restored to life, and he will see the Crucified and thank Him with immortal tongue.

On the day of the cross Christ saw some wondrous changes. The centurion who had superintended the driving of the nails became a believer; and one who had been crucified by His side became a believer. Can you think of cases that would appear more hopeless? A stranger from Africa; an officer in the Roman army whose callous heart had made him eligible for the post of superintendent of executioners; and one who was condemned to death, an inmate of death row!

But in the center of them all was the Man of Nazareth, praying, "Father, forgive." He had assured the world through His disciples, "I, if I be lifted up from the earth, will draw all men unto me." He was lifted up that men might come, and men were coming to Him.

He is lifted up before us that we might come to Him. Do you want to come too? Is the prayer of your heart "Lord, remember me"? Your Lord's petition for you is "Father, forgive." His promise to you is "Thou shalt be with Me in Paradise." Those about the cross could just as well have guaranteed themselves a place in Paradise as did the nameless thief of long ago. For each of these three converted men the deciding factor was the cross. One carried it, one nailed the Savior to it, and one died on a cross. The experiences of these three men may represent ours. I crucify the Son of God and put Him to open shame by my sins, as did the centurion. I should die with Jesus, as did the thief. But instead I must say with Paul, "I am crucified with Christ, nevertheless, I live." And I must accept my Master's word, "Take up your cross daily," as Simon did. But if through these experiences Jesus becomes my real master and I can say to Him, "Lord, remember me." His promise is for me, too. "Thou shalt be with Me in Paradise."

As we think of Christ and Him crucified, do we find it in our hearts to say, "Lord, take my life; take all of me. I wholly give myself to Thee"? Do you want to say this? If you do, I invite you to kneel down in quietness before the Savior and give your heart to Him. Confess your sins to Him. Beg Him for grace to help you to do what you ought to do. And all His gracious promises will be fulfilled in your life, and His peace will flood your heart.

Chapter 11

Mary the Consecrated

Woman Who Fell—"Rabboni"

Mary lived with Martha her sister and Lazarus her brother in Bethany, a village about one and one-half miles east of Jerusalem. To reach their home from Jerusalem, one would cross the Kiciron Valley and the summit of the Mount of Olives. Martha and Lazarus may have been joint owners of the house in which they lived, for we are told that Martha received Jesus "into her house" (Luke 10:38).

I would like to know more about Mary. Seven devils had been cast out of her (Luke 8:1, 2). Inspiration put its hand over her unhappy past. I wish we would do the same more often. I suspect that if we had been asked to tell the events of Mary's past we would have described each of those devils. God does not do that. As soon as He can He buries what He knows about us in a thick cloud. He does this, and why should we be willing to exhume a corpse? God sets us an example. We should put out of mind evil reports and records too. Our tongues are too ready to spread what is unpleasant. And our tongues, being so unpleasant themselves, make what is in itself unpleasant a thousand times worse by our exaggerations. May God exorcise this evil spirit from our souls.

We watch Martha and Mary and Lazarus together on a sunny afternoon, in company with Jesus and His disciples. Quite a house party Martha had! There were three residents and 13 visitors—at least 16 in all. Martha was distracted by all her duties, while

Mary sat at Jesus' feet (Luke 10:39). Jesus commended Mary's choice, declaring that she had chosen the "good part." He assured her that she would not be deprived of it. In passing, let us observe how our Lord addressed Martha (verse 41). "Jesus . . . said unto her, Martha, Martha . . ." The repetition of a name Jesus used on other occasions. This trait was revealed 18 centuries before. "Abraham, Abraham . . ." I hear it said again in His speeches: "Simon, Simon . . ."; "Jerusalem, Jerusalem . . ."

Let us gather together the facts in our story. In our first picture of Mary we see someone out of whose heart God has cast seven devils (Luke 8:1, 2). She has come back home. Perhaps, because of her wandering, she is slightly resented by Martha. She takes up some of the household chores, but she is determined that she will fulfill that "good part," and "also" sit at her Master's feet and learn of Him. Nothing must be allowed to separate her from her Lord.

Everything was now all right between them. Why did Mary need to hear Christ's words further? we might inquire. Life was wonderful; why did she need to pray now? I don't know whether Mary asked those questions or whether she even thought such thoughts; but some of us do. Whenever everything is going along just right, we pray less. When the sun is shining, we don't feel we need an umbrella! We do not even think about a raincoat. But then it begins to pour! Mary, however, did think ahead. She had discovered that there was a "good part" at the feet of Jesus. This she resolved would be hers.

The second picture the New Testament writers present of Mary has its setting in a day of gloom (John 11:1ff.). The sun has gone out behind a very dark cloud. It is pouring! A terrible tragedy has stuck the little family. Lazarus is desperately sick. The sisters send an urgent request for their Pastor. But the Pastor does not come immediately. It is always hard for a family facing a crisis when the pastor does not come.

And Lazarus died, and they closed his eyes, folded his hands, wrapped him in a linen shroud, and carried him to a cave just outside Bethany and buried him, and put a stone across the entrance and came back to an empty home and waited, and the Pastor did not come even then.

And the next day the Pastor did not come. Then four days after Lazarus had been taken to the tomb, the Pastor came. But there was no Lazarus to visit. There were only Martha and Mary and an empty house with empty hearts. And when Martha heard that Jesus was there she came to Him, and with grief surging in her heart said, "If thou hadst been here, my brother had not died." And Jesus in effect said, "Martha, believe. I am the resurrection and the life. A man who is dead may live again." Then Jesus sent her back with a message: "Tell Mary I am here."

If those who are bereaved will carry to others the message that Jesus is near, they themselves will be comforted. And now Mary came at once. And as we watch, Mary falls at the feet of Jesus. This choice had been her habitual one in the day of sunshine, so she naturally went to Jesus in the day of shadow.

"Jesus wept," and, weeping, went to the tomb's entrance—Martha still arguing about how improper this would be—and called the brother to life. That must have been a very happy evening. There is no record that Jesus stayed. The family had been reunited. They had so much to talk over, so much for which to be thankful. And so Jesus withdrew.

And in the next chapter of John (12:1ff.) we watch a Sabbath dinner. This was the last Sabbath dinner that Jesus had before His crucifixion. It was quite a big dinner party, and was held at the house of Simon the Pharisee. Martha was there, serving in somebody else's house (John 12:2). Capable, organizing, successful at her task, born leader that she was, she was captain of every kitchen into which she moved. And then John added, "Lazarus was one of them that sat at the table with him." That is the happiest place for a man at a Sabbath dinner, anyway—sitting in anticipation! Jesus was in the group, too, talking with His friends.

Suddenly there stole upon the guests a rich perfume. It filled the whole room. They looked about and saw Mary at the feet of Jesus. I often wonder what a pastor today would do if some member of his congregation came, while he was at table on Sabbath, and poured perfume over his feet. We don't do things like that now. They didn't do things like that then either, not very often—but Mary did!

This dinner party was in Simon's house. Influenced by Judas, Simon criticized Mary's act. He said in his heart, "This man, if he were a prophet, would have known who and what manner of woman this is that toucheth him: for she is a sinner" (Luke 7:39). Jesus took in the scene clearly. He had met the leading characters before. "By curing Simon of leprosy, Christ had saved him from a living death" (*The Desire of Ages,* p. 566). But Simon had not been grateful. What memories must have crowded Simon's mind at that moment. The woman by the feet of Jesus was one he immediately recognized, but whom he had tried to forget. "Simon had led into sin the woman he now despised. She had been deeply wronged by him" (*ibid.*). He knew she was a sinner, for he had been her seducer!

Then Jesus looked at him, and said, "Simon, I have somewhat to say unto you." The blood must have drained from his face, for he probably surmised that Jesus knew his past. In a hoarse voice he replied, "Master, say on." And then Christ told the story of the two debtors. His conclusion was that he loves most who has been forgiven most. "As did Nathan with David, Christ concealed His home thrust under the veil of a parable" (*ibid.*). He now knew he needed much forgiveness. "Simon was touched by the kindness of Jesus in not openly rebuking him before the guests. . . . His pride was humbled, he repented, and the proud Pharisee became a lowly, self-sacrificing disciple" (*ibid., p.* 568).

Then Christ promised that wherever the gospel should be preached, this story would be told about Mary. I am telling you Mary's story and so am fulfilling our Lord's prophecy. She had a good reason for doing this to her Savior. She wanted to tell Jesus that she was giving Him His wreath, His gift of love, before His death. Her insight showed her the shortening shadows of His cross. She sensed that in the immediate future Jesus would die. I wonder which offering Christ preferred, Mary's gift of one pound of spikenard during that Sabbath dinner the week before His death, or the 100 pounds of spikenard from Nicodemus on the evening of His burial? Which one do you think warmed His heart more? With one He was thrilled, encouraged; about the other, He was later told. A boutonniere for someone alive is better than a bouquet to him dead! And so Jesus commended Mary, this woman whom He had cleansed from sin, who through the months had sat at His feet and chosen the better part, and trusted and prayed, to whom the Spirit had given rich insights.

On that awful Friday Mary sobbed at the cross. There was nothing else she could do, and so she wept for her Beloved. She lingered near Him, until darkness hid His form. She heard Him pray. She watched Him die as the curtain was lifted and the glory of the throne enveloped His form. She tried to help them take Him down from the cross. She helped wrap the sheets and arrange Him in the tomb. And then she cried herself to sleep.

On the Resurrection morning Christ delayed His return to His Father because of Mary. During the Friday's darkness His soul had cried out, "Why hast thou forsaken me?" The separation was breaking His heart. Yet on the Sunday morning He did not ascend immediately to His Father. He knew that groping in the shadows of the garden was a woman, weeping because she loved.

The gates of Paradise were wide open for the risen Christ. The angel choirs, "ten thousand times ten thousand, and thousands of thousands," had been practicing their anthems for this triumphal moment. The guard of honor was lining the shining path through space along which Jesus would return to His Father's home. The Father longed for this reunion with His Son. From the heights above He eagerly watched for His coming. From a long way off He was ready to run and throw His arms about Him. His joyous cry was about to ring through the universe, "This My Son was dead and is alive! Give Him the robe of divinity and the ring of authority. Rejoice with Me. He who never strayed was lost for those who were lost. He who knew no sin became sin for those who sinned. And now He is coming back." But the Father waited. And the choir director waited. And the guard of honor waited. All this was because that stumbling, sobbing, sinful, cleansed woman was looking for Jesus in the garden. And then as she wept, and thought she saw the gardener, she heard Christ's voice say, "Mary!" And then she bowed in adoration at His feet. That one word brought back to her soul transports of worshipful joy as she fell at the feet of Jesus.

"Not yet, Mary, not yet," Jesus warned. Mary's place was ever at His feet worshipping in the day of sunshine; at His feet trusting in the hour of sorrow; at His feet doing the simple service she could because of Calvary; at His feet at the foot of the cross; and now at His feet on this Resurrection morn.

And then upon the lips of one from whom seven devils had been cast, Jesus Christ put the message of His resurrection. To her, and to her only, He declared that He was about to return to His Father, and hers! The scribes and Pharisees might question. Judas, the traitor, might betray. The disciples might wonder. Martha might criticize. Her own friends might laugh. But what did all that matter when by her habit of consecration to Christ, heart to heart, soul to soul, insight to insight, understanding to understanding, she was bound by the cords of unbreakable love to her Master forever? Nothing mattered to Mary because of that relationship.

On the day of the resurrection I want to hear the Gardener say to me, "Leslie!" Then I want to fall at His feet with the cry of dedication, "Rabboni, Master!" Mary the consecrated has left me a shining example.

Chapter 12

Mary the Virgin

Woman Who Shared—"How May This Be?"

Our story begins in a tiny village in Galilee. Everyone knew everyone else better than they knew themselves. Everyone's business was conducted by everyone else more successfully than by the one who was conducting it. It is always like that in little villages, and it was like that in Nazareth. Nazareth was probably a very unpleasant place in which to preach. I am thankful I am not preaching in Nazareth. I would not relish the prospect of being thrown into the creek by those who disagree with me! The town had such an evil reputation that the question arose naturally, "Can any good thing come out of Nazareth?" Actually, the best Person in the world came out of Nazareth. But the world didn't know it then, and they certainly didn't know it in Nazareth.

Somewhere in that little village was a carpenter's shop. It was run by a sad-faced widower. He had boys at home for whom he had to earn a living. Like some young boys, they weren't the nicest fellows, but they were his boys, and he had to feed them. There were one or two girls, too. But things weren't looking quite so black, because a young woman in Nazareth had agreed to share his home and his responsibilities with him. For this reason the sun was shining a little more brightly, and the birds were twittering a little more sweetly, and the shavings were curling off the lumber a little more pleasantly, and the saw was singing a merry song. Life looked much better. Joseph had put a ring around a special day in his diary. It was his wedding date.

She lived down the street, and her heart was singing too. Mary was looking forward to that day as all women look forward to their wedding date. And then without any warning, something, as sudden as a bombshell, exploded.

An angel came and talked to Mary. It was strange talk—it was heaven's talk. "Blessed art thou among women" (Luke 1:28). Of all the women in all the world, in all the ages, God had chosen Mary and submerged her in His grace. Of all the responsibilities of all the women in all the ages, God gave to Mary the most exciting task. And of all the messengers that He might have sent from all heaven, He chose Gabriel. And Gabriel came to Mary with that startling message. With no announcement, with no conditioning, he stood in front of her and told her what God expected her to do. It was something (and I have looked for this word carefully) that was *fantastic*—with all that that word means. It was unbelievable; it was impossible. Nothing like that had ever happened; nothing like that has ever happened since; nothing like that will ever happen again. And Gabriel stood before the maid of Nazareth and told her that she was to have a baby who was to be God. And that simple girl accepted the challenge.

Mary eagerly inquired, "How?" Not in the way Nicodemus asked Christ "How?" on that dark night outside Jerusalem. His "How?" was full of doubt; he expected the answer "Impossible!" His "How?" had overtones of "Don't be silly. An old man with all his habit patterns formed, with his way of life crystallized through years of experience! How can he go back and start again? He is a product of all his yesterdays." It wasn't a question like that that Mary asked. It was a question a child might ask if you said someone was waiting with $10 if a certain condition was fulfilled. He or she would settle down in your lap and ask excitedly, "What can I do? How can I get it?" There was longing in Mary's "How?"

There was belief in that "How?" There was trust in that "How?" And there was reliance that what she couldn't do herself God could do. And the angel's answer is as mysterious as it is simple. "The Holy Ghost shall come upon thee, and the power of the Highest shall overshadow thee: therefore also that holy thing which shall be born of thee shall be called the Son of God" (verse 35). Like so many things in life, it is disarmingly simple, and it is designed by its simplicity to disarm. Mary's response is one that I want to fix in your memory forever. If you forget all the accidentals of this biographical portrayal, if you remember nothing else I say, don't forget this. It is the most important word I can tell you. It was the reply of Mary 1900 years ago: "Behold the handmaid of the Lord; be it unto me according to thy word" (verse 38). Every problem in your life will be solved if you will say that as Mary said it.

Some of us have aches in our hearts. These come because of something we have done; sometimes, because of something the world has done to us. As we sit in church, we think of yesterday or the night before, of what we did last week, and our hearts are pained. We so terribly regret what we said or what we did or what we didn't say or what we didn't do or what we were or what we should have been and weren't. Do you want a solution for your problem? Do you long for peace in your heart? Do you wish to grasp the certainty that God is ruling in your life and guiding you and taking you to the green pastures of His celestial fields? Do you really want these? Then you must give yourself to God without reservation. Do you want Jesus to live in your heart? Do you want Christ to be formed in you? Do you want to present the Savior to your family? to your neighbors? to your friends? Then this, too, you must affirm: "Behold the handmaid of the Lord; be it unto me according to thy word."

And suddenly Gabriel had gone. A moment before, his effulgence was shining around the girl of Nazareth and making the sun seem dim. But now he is gone, and Mary is alone with her secret. And what a secret! How would she explain it! She couldn't explain it in Nazareth. She could already see the supercilious smile curling upon the lips of Nazareth. She couldn't tell it to Joseph. How could he understand? And then one day she had to tell it to Joseph. There was nothing else she could do. Even Joseph would see, and she must tell him before he could see. And Joseph was deeply hurt. He took out his diary and rubbed off that date. He felt it was just a dream that had gone sour. And Joseph's hurt hurt Mary. She hoped he would understand, but he didn't. She thought he might, but he couldn't.

Possibly it was then that she remembered what Gabriel had told her. "Thy cousin Elisabeth . . ." Yes, she knew something about her cousin. Elisabeth lived somewhere near Hebron, in the hills of Judea. She was not as young as Mary. She had lived in another world, but now she and Mary had something in common. They each had a secret, an angel-announced secret. Mary set off on the journey southward, stumbling and wondering and hurrying. On her way she passed Jerusalem. There was Gethsemane, but for this she had no eyes. And then there was Calvary, but the sword had not yet entered into her heart, although she could feel its point. And by it there was Olivet with the vision glorious of her Son rising to His Father, but she couldn't see that yet. And then she was at Elisabeth's home, and they talked and understood and drew nearer to each other and nearer to God.

I like to imagine that back in Nazareth Joseph went to the synagogue. Church is the best place to go to be uplifted. Perhaps the preacher read out what the prophet said: "Behold, a virgin shall conceive." Joseph had heard these words many times before, but they hadn't meant a thing to him. Then the thought became real. A virgin conceive! I don't think he heard anything more that morning. A virgin had conceived. Could it be? Seven hundred years ago the prophecy had been made. And now he had seen it fulfilled! "O God, forgive me for my doubt and unbelief," he must have prayed that day.

He stumbled out of the synagogue and greeted the leader, but nothing of this meant anything to him. He must be alone, he must pray, and then Gabriel was with him to comfort and assure him.

Perhaps the celestial messenger talked to him like this: 'Don't be afraid, Joseph; marry the girl. This is the fulfillment of the prophecy. You're older than she. She needs you. She needs you more than you know." And I can see, in my imagination, Joseph stumbling over those hills and going down to Judea. There he met Zacharias. And those two men were both angel warned and angel scolded. Zacharias, the priest, and Joseph, the carpenter, had their secret too. Only they couldn't talk about it. Joseph had to do all the talking. Zacharias had to get out his pad and write, "That's just how I felt. I didn't believe, and look what happened to me." And Joseph would say, "I didn't believe, and look what happened to me."

And I like to think that Joseph and Mary went back to Nazareth together. And, oh, how different that road back must have been! Now they both shared a secret. They both realized that they both had been talked to by Gabriel. And they both had a joyous responsibility. And they both had a task to fulfill. And so they went back hand in hand. And the birds were singing again, and the sun was shining again, and joy was bubbling in their hearts again. And later the hard trip to Bethlehem wasn't so hard, because Joseph and Mary were together.

And then Jesus was born. There is no record of Joseph's saying anything when the shepherds came. He didn't need to say anything. He was there beaming and happy. When the shepherds told the story about the angels' song, Joseph thought he could hear the voice of Gabriel in that chorus. And then he went up to the Temple with Mary and Jesus. The priest picked up that little Babe, and Joseph was there smiling and happy. He heard the strange words: "A sword shall pierce through thine own soul also." But he didn't really hear them. They weren't for him, and he soon forgot them. But not so the maid of Nazareth. She stored those burning phrases in her heart. And then came hard days when a price was put on the head of the Babe and the soldiers were looking for Him and the little donkey could only go so slowly to Egypt. Joseph must have had to buy some tools in that faraway land and begin again to toil for three hungry mouths. And then came the happy rumor and the happier dream. And soon they were on the trip back. And the housekeeping began in Nazareth. The little Boy grew till He was 12. And they went to the Temple and lost Him! And the little Boy talked about His Father's house and His Father's business. And the years slipped away.

Then in Cana there is a wedding, and Jesus is there. Mary is there too. Mary is happy to be there. Her Boy is a wonderful boy.

At the wedding wine is needed, and the host looks to Mary, and she looks to her Boy. He whispers strange words: "Mine hour is not yet come." Did she see the uplifted hand? Did she see the cup and the wine? Did she sense the hour with its throbbing pain and its open fountain and the new covenant in His blood? Did she understand? She goes back to the servants at the banquet and says, "Whatsoever he saith unto you, do it." Those words of Mary I leave with you today. Never forget them.

Then we see her standing at the foot of the cross. We watch

her faint. We see the strong arms of John pick her up and take her to his home. I went to Ephesus and saw the traditional place where she is said later to have lived, and the hill on which she is said to have been buried. I don't know whether the tradition is fact, but I relived her story. I imagined Mary, an old woman, talking to John and listening to his messages, because John loved and she loved, and they were united by the One they loved.

Mary's words come to us just as movingly now as they came in days gone by. Two words they are—one about herself, and one to us. Here is the first: "Behold the handmaid of the Lord; be it unto me according to thy word." Her consecration sustained and carried her beyond Calvary to rest at last awaiting glory. The other is the motto of her life: "Whatsoever he saith unto you, do it." That was her gospel as she gave us Jesus Christ. And if Paul were here today he would cry, "I travail in birth again until Christ be formed in you" (Gal. 4:19). This is my appeal, for I too have prayed that Christ be formed in you.

The angel Gabriel does not stand in front of you and tell you of your destiny, but the Holy Spirit does. Here and now you may hear another voice, not mine, but the voice of the Spirit deep down in your heart. The whole creation is waiting for a revelation of the Son of God in you, groaning and travailing in anticipation. We hear the heart cry of the world on every radio broadcast. We read its sobbing story in every newspaper. People are waiting for a manifestation of the Son of God. We are to present Him to them.

"Christ be formed in you." Do you wish it? "Behold the handslave of the Lord; be it unto me according to thy word." must be your response. Will you say that? God help you to say it now. For until you reach that point and become His slave; until you reach the place where you can say, "Be it unto me according to thy word," you have a long way to go. But when you say it, you have arrived. Jesus lives in your heart. And thereafter your motto will also be "Whatsoever He says unto me, I will do it."

If you have never given yourself, body, soul, and spirit to Jesus, do it now. Do it because He loves, and loves you yesterday, today, and all the tomorrows. Give yourself to Him. The virgin Mary blazed the trail. It took a sword that pierced her soul. Her example is ours.

Chapter 13

Jesus the Crucified

Man Who Died—God Who Wept

On the central cross Jesus the sorrowing died that we might live. I want you to think about three dramatic moments in His life that led to Calvary. They reveal His character and demonstrate that there was no alternative to His sacrificial death. Let us travel back in imagination to the beginning.

The world had just been created. The Father, the Son, and the Spirit had taken their flight from somewhere in illimitable space where their throne is. They had come to the part of the universe that was to be occupied by this planet. Then Jesus, the Eternal Word, spoke, and a world was born! Hurled at incredible speed and with tremendous momentum, it began its continuing orbit along the pathway God assigned to it.

Christ then called light into being. He invited the dry land to appear. He whispered to the grass, and it clothed the fields. He talked to the trees, and they lifted up their arms to caress the skies. As the gentle winds stirred them, He designed them as cradles for the birds that sing and the animals that scamper. And in their shade the beasts of the field rested. Fish darted in the waters, and butterflies searched for goblets of nectar in each fragrant blossom. All the world was very beautiful.

And after His six days' work, God looked at each thing His hands had formed, and "behold, it was very good." This was especially true of the man He had just sculptured from the dust—Adam, the crown and the monument of His creation. He was the center of his Father's love, the seed of His ambition. Man stood before his Maker in all his God-bestowed majesty, able to communicate and love and worship. As the afternoon shadows lengthened on that Friday, Adam slept in the quietness of some forest dell. He had spent a busy morning naming the creatures. From his side the creative fingers of the creative Christ had taken a bone. This He had fashioned into Eve, man's companion, his counterpart, his lover, and his beloved. And hand in hand they walked through the fragrant glades and listened to the chorus of praise that ascended from every moving, every living thing on this planet. Theirs were the first ears that could hear to understand, and the first eyes that could see to perceive. And Adam and Eve must have joined their voices as a sacred obligato to the hymns of adoration that all creation raised to its Creator. Then "God rested," not as one wearied, but as one utterly satisfied with the works of His hands.

But forming a background to this happy episode was another—sinister, darkly dramatic. In the heaven of heavens rebellion had already taken place. He who, next to Christ, had been the greatest had yielded to the corrosive stir of envy within his soul. Conscious of his own worth, cognizant of the inferiority of many about him, Lucifer was ambitious for his own glory. But his was an ambition that would brook no curb. With a guilty vision of power, whose uses he could not fathom, he demanded equality with Christ Himself. Long and insidiously he presented his arguments to the angelic hosts. Long and patiently the Father waited. But at last the storm, which could be no longer restrained, broke with all its fury.

Where there had been peace, there was now war. Where there had been praise, there was now curse. Where there had been love, there was now hate. Where the sons of God had sung in joy, the warriors of the adversary struggled in rage. There could be only one outcome to that war. Satan was expelled headlong from heaven with his host of rebellious, unrepentant angels.

And now the two episodes we have noted come together. The holy pair in Eden were in a holy environment in a holy world. And into that holy garden Satan projected an unholy thought. Because he hated Christ, he hated everything that was Christ's. Because he hated holiness, he hated everything that was holy. Because he hated the Father, he hated His children. So he considered what he should do.

Adam and Eve were sinless. Satan understood the conditions upon which their righteousness depended. He knew that only at the tree of the knowledge of good and evil was he permitted to make an approach to them. Only at that place did he have any possibility of success. A short time before he had led the choirs in praise; now the angels, who were his minions, were quarreling bitterly. Before there had been songs of triumph; now there were cries of frenzy. Ellen G. White paints this moving picture of the scene: "These spirits had become turbulent with disappointed hopes. Instead of greater good, they were experiencing the sad results of disobedience and disregard of the law. Never more would these unhappy beings be swayed by the mild rule of Jesus Christ. Never more would their spirits be stirred by the deep, earnest love, peace, and joy which His presence had ever inspired in them.

"Satan trembled as he viewed his work. He was alone in meditation upon the past, the present, and his future plans. His mighty frame shook as with a tempest. An angel from heaven was passing. He called him and entreated an interview with Christ. This was granted him. He then related to the Son of God that he repented of his rebellion and wished again the favor of God. He was willing to take the place God had previously assigned him, and be under His wise command." Now, notice the inspired sentence which follows: "Christ wept at Satan's woe but told him, as the mind of God, that he could never be received into heaven. Heaven must not be placed in jeopardy" (*The Story of Redemption,* pp. 25, 26).

I want you to see this scene clearly. Consider carefully this encounter of the created with his Creator. Lucifer, "the son of the morning," the bearer of light, now turned into the prince of darkness, faces Jesus Christ, the Creator of light. Michael confronts Satan. And Satan senses the consequences of his rebellion. He knows he has forfeited his position in heaven. He realizes the abyss to which his mind is now taking him. He is actually contemplating the seduction and destruction of the innocents in the Garden of Eden. He is horrified at his own thoughts and longs to undo what he has already done, but, because of the implications of his activities, he feels it is now too late. He is certain that he can no more return to his former love of God. His thoughts have finally crystallized into rebellion. Never again will the warming, melting appeals of his King soften his heart and those of his followers and absorb them within divine light and truth and love.

And Christ, seeing His enemy's anguish, weeps. I want you to focus on that thought. Then allow your mind to roam across the vista of the centuries yet unborn. Jesus could actually weep at Satan's woe! Knowing that tomorrow or the next tomorrow the devil would break the communion between Adam and Eve and their Creator; knowing that soon the blood of Abel would stain this perfect planet with the mark of the first murder; knowing that centuries later this earth would be so steeped in evil that only the waters from the windows of heaven could wash it clean and make it possible to begin again with a little family of those who were still righteous; in spite of all this, Jesus could weep for Satan. This passes my comprehension.

Our Savior looked over all the battlefields of all the ages. He heard the dying sob of dying men. He listened to the crying moan of crying mothers, and yet He wept at the anguish of the being who had yet not done what he planned to do! And Jesus saw Gethsemane, and He saw Golgotha. He saw what Satan would do to Him when He was defenseless because of love; when He was powerless because of sacrifice.

Then Christ would take the place of men and women to die at the hand of Satan. Jesus looked at him who would do all this and more, for in all the bleeding, crying centuries that have followed Calvary, iniquity has increased through Satan's efforts; and He wept for him.

Jesus saw the battlefields, where millions of men bled and died, the blood-drenched fields of Flanders, where today the crimson poppies bloom, Stalingrad, Hiroshima. And He looked beyond. And still He wept—wept at the misery of him who was the architect of all this misery. Can you understand sympathy like this? Can you imagine loving an enemy like this? When He stood on that nameless hill, with the multitudes before Him that summer day 19 centuries ago, He said to them, "Love your enemies, bless them that curse you, do good to them that hate you, and pray for them which despitefully use you, and persecute you" and for those who "say all manner of evil against you falsely" (Matt. 5:44, 11). He was talking from the depths of His experience. He Himself thus loved—loved with an everlasting, overmastering love. And when "the morning stars sang together, and all the sons of God shouted for joy," and the angel choirs poured forth praises to their Creator, because their insights and visions were not as far-reaching as His,

Christ wept for Satan's sorrow. And now we leave His tears and pass on in our meditation.

And the years go by and iniquity multiplies, and men and women flood the world with vice and crime. Conditioned by the adversary, they now seek to outdo him in sinning. God had made them perfect, but they invent to themselves all manner of evil things. And the centuries lengthen into millenniums, until He who sits enthroned afar sees that iniquity has reached its depths. The nadir has been plumbed. Evil spirits control the brains and the nerves and the muscles and the organs of men and women to do evil. The fullness of time has come. The clock of heaven has struck. And to the maid of Nazareth there comes the messenger from the Invisible. To her heart there wings the Infinite to dwell in the utterly finite. The Creator came on His way to earth. He stooped as low as He was able. He emptied Himself as fully as He could. He came, bent low to enter the door into humanity. He came when the world was filled with 4,000 years of sin; when men had practiced 4,000 years of evil.

But He came. And at last men saw Him as a babe in a stable. He came, and at last the young couples of Nazareth, just setting up home, coveted the furniture He made. And the farmers in the fields vied with one another to get in line for the plows He fashioned. The world has no record of the material things He did, because His was not a kingdom that might be seen, of which men might say, "Lo here, and lo there." He left no shrine, no monument that men might touch, because His was a kingdom of the spirit. He came that death might be dispelled with life. He came that hatred might give place to love. He came to undo all that Satan has done.

We watch Him move from village to village. And the healing of the seamless dress, the healing of that creative Hand, the healing of that omnipotent Word, restored whole towns so that there was not a single sick person in them. We follow Him as He moves, unassuming, quiet, and genial, from hamlet to hamlet, from city to city. We observe Him trudge the mountaintop to preach or pray. We see Him descend the valley to comfort or heal. We note His journey over the hills to the coasts of Tyre and Sidon because outside the confines of Israel His heart had felt the turmoil of another heart in need; we hear Him speak peace to a mother in a heathen land. And everywhere men sing and women wipe away their tears and children laugh because He passed.

And then one day we see Him climb the hills of Galilee and go southward to Jerusalem, and east to a little village lying on the slope of Olivet. They could easily be missed—perhaps these 20 or 30 homes, the color of the brown hills, flat-roofed, one-story buildings. Not far away is a cave, and the cave is His goal. Jesus and the twelve go to Bethany. The way is barred a moment by Martha's anguish and Mary's tears. But at last He reaches the place He wants to be. He stands outside a cavern where Lazarus lies. And standing about Christ in the sunlight, Martha weeps and Mary sobs, the dead man's friends are not dry-eyed, and the professional mourners cry in simulated grief.

Jesus had to come to Bethany because He looked beyond the tomb. He saw Lazarus alive again. He saw his bed at home occupied by a calmly sleeping, healthy man. Jesus could look ahead and see the triumphal procession into Jerusalem with the strong hand of a resurrected Lazarus guiding the donkey He rode. He could see his resurrection. To Him it was only minutes away. But when He saw sorrow that could not see; when He felt grief that had no eyes; when He grasped faithlessness that could not pierce the darkness that shrouded it and discerned only the sorrow clutching at the hearts of blind and helpless and faithless men, Jesus wept.

For whom were these tears of God? Jesus wept for those whose loved ones sleep, who have gone the last walk and have come back alone because they do not sense that Christ is there. He weeps for all who do not believe.

"Jesus wept." John explains much that Jesus did, but he makes no attempt to explain this act. The shortest verse in the Bible has the longest meaning. Jesus actually sympathized with sorrow that would give place to joy in five minutes. He was so anguished that men should suffer even for a little while, that "Jesus wept."

And then Lazarus was called forth, and Martha threw her arms about him, and Mary clung to him in affection. But Jesus had gone. Perhaps to Gethsemane, perhaps down by Kidron, perhaps even farther south, lost in a bend of the road, in a fold of the dun-colored hills of Judea, Jesus went alone to contemplate His plan and humanity's reaction. Jesus wept for humanity's sorrow. And so we leave His tears and pass on in our meditation.

The weeks quickly slip by. The climax of Christ's life is about to break. And then one day Jesus calls two of His disciples and says, in effect, Go into that village, and you will find a donkey and its foal. Go in—bring them. And if anyone inquires, say "The Master has need," and it will be enough. And they went, and they found as He had said, did as He had bidden, and came as He had required. And the disciples put their robes upon the back of the little animal, and Christ mounted.

Then they began the journey to Jerusalem. Never had the people beheld a sight like this. Over those hills and across those valleys His dusty feet had carried Jesus all those years. He had walked as a servant, but now He rode as a prince. The disciples thought that something important was in the air. It was less than a week before the Passover. The name of Lazarus was on many a lip. He had been dead for so long. The evidence of his resurrection was so obvious. There was no doubt that this was a miracle. Perhaps some of the people coming up to Passover arrived early so as to see Lazarus. And so they came—hundreds of thousands of men and women. Josephus tells us that there were occasionally between 2 and 3 million people who attended the Passover at Jerusalem in the first century. Who knows how many millions were there, spilling across the hills and valleys for miles around Jerusalem, their low, black tents, like the tents of the Bedouin today, sheltering their families for the week's pilgrimage.

Many of these join Christ and His disciples in a vast triumphal procession. Slowly the throng climbs the Mount of Olives and traverses its top toward Jerusalem. Rounding a bend in the road, the people see the city spread out before them.

"While the westering sun was tinting and gilding the heavens, its resplendent glory lighted up the pure white marble of the Temple walls, and sparkled on its gold-capped pillars. From the crest of the hill where Jesus and His followers stood, it had the appearance of a massive structure of snow, set with golden pinnacles. At the entrance to the Temple was a vine of gold and silver, with green leaves and massive clusters of grapes executed by the most skillful artists. This design represented Israel as a prosperous vine. The gold, silver, and living green were combined with rare taste and exquisite workmanship. As it twined gracefully about the white and glistening pillars, clinging with shining tendrils to their golden ornaments, it caught the splendor of the setting sun, shining as if with a glory borrowed from heaven.

"Jesus gazes upon the scene, and the vast multitude hush their shouts, spellbound by the sudden vision of beauty. All eyes turn upon the Savior, expecting to see in His countenance the admiration they themselves feel. But instead of this they behold a cloud of sorrow. They are surprised and disappointed to see His eyes fill with tears, and His body rock to and fro like a tree before the tempest, while a wail of anguish bursts from His quivering lips, as if from the depths of a broken heart. What a sight was this for angels to behold! their loved Commander in an agony of tears. What a sight was this for the glad throng that with shouts of triumph and the waving of palm branches were escorting Him to the glorious city, where they fondly hoped He was about to reign! Jesus had wept at the grave of Lazarus, but it was in a God-like grief in sympathy with human woe. But this sudden sorrow was like a note of wailing in a grand triumphal chorus. In the midst of a scene of rejoicing, where all were paying Him homage, Israel's King was in tears; not silent tears of gladness, but tears and groans of insuppressible agony. The multitude were struck with a sudden gloom. Their acclamations were silenced. Many wept in sympathy with a grief they could not comprehend" (*The Desire of Ages,* pp. 575, 576).

Jesus did not weep for His own sorrow, even though Gethsemane lay at His feet. He did not weep for His own anguish, though Calvary stood just outside the city wall. He did not weep for His own death, although His tomb was by Golgotha. He wept for Jerusalem, the city that for centuries had been the type and symbol of God's chosen people, but that had rejected the Savior and was about to crucify its King. And in those tears He included us who turn our backs on His proffered mercy and spurn His loving appeals. His tears are for us today who live when Heaven is about to declare to the world, as Christ declared to Jerusalem, "Behold, your house is left unto you desolate."

But Christ had inspired the sweet singer of Israel to record, 10 centuries before, the philosophy by which the kingdom of

God is established. "They that sow in tears shall reap in joy" (Ps. 126:5). Now He was sowing the Word in human soil. The seeds were being wet by His loving tears and given life by His precious blood. The divine Husbandman was toiling toward His great harvest. Some seeds fell on the highways of life, and the vultures of greed and the hawks of materialism snatched them away before they struck down their roots. Some seeds fell among the stones that hurt His legs and bruised His body and held the seeds back from their normal growth. But some seed fell on good soil and grew and flourished and brought forth much fruit. And the Husbandman was glad that He had sowed and that He had wept. And His voice was heard in joyous proclamation: "The Lord thy God in the midst of thee is mighty; he will save, he will rejoice over thee with joy; he will rest in his love, he will joy over thee with singing" (Zeph. 3:17).

On the great harvest day the Great Harvester will rejoice over His harvest with a song of harvest home.

When the morning stars sang to celebrate Creation Christ wept at Satan's woe. When the sister remonstrated with Jesus about opening the grave, Christ wept. When the multitudes sang to honor the triumphal entry of the Messiah, Christ wept at Jerusalem's woe. And when the controversy ends and Jesus gathers the elect, the wicked will weep in anguish and remorse. But in the earth made new our Savior will lead the redeemed through gardens His hands have planted, to mansions He has furnished, into His Father's house in which He lives. And then He will rejoice over His bride with singing. Lost in His love, joying in His victory, thrilled with His beloved, He will burst into song.

Will you be there when Christ sings His solo?

Conclusion

A nd for a moment we shall linger yet about the cross and look at the faces of those who watched the Son of God die. No longer are they so unknown. No longer are they strangers, shadows of anonymous men and women. They are we. We are watching Christ executed as surely as if we were on Golgotha 1900 years ago. We see Christ, the Prince of heaven, the Son of man, our Elder Brother, our Substitute and Surety, dying on our behalf on Calvary's tree. Old Skull Face no longer leers at us. Golgotha is vital for our salvation. It puts a song of appreciation in our hearts.

Some of these who watched Christ executed were unmoved by the viewing, or were moved to final hatred and rejection. There were Pilate, pathetic in his craven pliability; Herod, bombastic, trapped by his own lips; Caiaphas, cynical religionist, burnt by the flame of his own unholy ambition; and Judas, mixed up in his misplaced zeal, dragged to death by the weight of 30 coins. These men came face to face with Christ on the cross and destroyed Him, each in his own way, and by that destruction destroyed themselves. Then there were others, Simon the Cyrenian, conscripted to carry the cross, consecrated to this task forever with joyous abandon; Nicodemus the cautious, eventually boldly championing his Lord; Peter the boastful, transformed into the preacher of Pentecost; John Thunderson changed into the beloved; Mary, the hold of seven vile spirits, born into the surrendered evangel of the resurrection; the centurion the conscientious, sensing the just among the unjust; the thief struggling in pain on Jerusalem's trash heap and scaling the walls of Paradise; and Mary the maid presenting to us the Babe of Bethlehem. All these came face to face with Christ and destroyed self, each in his own way. And by that destruction gained salvation for themselves.

And on the cross the Crucified died, "a Man of sorrows," that He might put a song in our hearts and praise on our lips and life in our vile bodies. And in the hour of His apparent defeat He gained the greatest victory of every age for those of us who will accept Him, and it.

What are you going to do about this Man Christ Jesus? In the final count all the problems of your life may be resolved at this point. Peace and joy and life on the one hand, and conflict and pain and death on the other, meet their watershed on Calvary. I appeal to each of you to decide for Christ. Christ, God's Son, has been executed for you, by you. Yet God is setting before you what is best. Choose it now and live, in time and in eternity. And sing, at last, "the song of the Lamb."

OTHER EXCITING STORIES
IN THE FAMILY FAVORITES SERIES

STRANGERS IN THE LAND
Louise A. Vernon

...yone who refused to convert ...ould be imprisoned, and the dragoons had orders to kill anyone who tried to escape. Paperback.

THE SWORD OF DENIS ANWYCK
Maylan Schurch
Paperback.

NEW!

THE GATES SERIES
by Thurman C. Petty, Jr.

SIEGE AT THE GATES
The Story of Sennacherib, Hezekiah, and Isaiah
Paperback, 160 pages.

THE TEMPLE GATES
The Story of Josiah, Jedidah, and Judah's Idolatry
Paperback, 144 pages.

FIRE IN THE GATES
The Story of Nebuchadnezzar, Jeremiah, and Baruch
Paperback, 112 pages.

GATE OF THE GODS
The Story of Daniel, Nebuchadnezzar, and Loyalty to God
Paperback, 128 pages.

THE OPEN GATES
The Story of Cyrus, Daniel, and Darius
Paperback, 176 pages.